*Thomas M. Murphy*

# Successful Selling For Introverts

*Achieving Sales Success without a Traditional Sales Personality*

Sheba Press
Portland, Oregon

Successful Selling For Introverts: Achieving Sales Success without a Traditional Sales Personality

Copyright © 1999 by Thomas M. Murphy

**Sheba Press**
1165 NW 178th Ave.
Beaverton, OR 970065
(503) 516-3193
Fax (503) 629-9852

Book production by Cypress House, Fort Bragg, CA 95437

ISBN 0-9662286-0-X

Printed in U.S.A.

First edition

*This book would not have been possible without the love and understanding of my wife Deborah, my son Tim and my daughter Meghan. Deborah served as my editor and added numerous comments and insights throughout the book. I dedicate this book to them for their patience and encouragement.*

# How to use this Book

*Successful Selling for Introverts* is designed to be read and re-read, referenced and used throughout your career. Selling is a dynamic, turbulent, exciting part of any business. One day you can be on top of the world – and the next day you wonder whatever possessed you to think you could persuade anyone to buy your product or service. We're going to address the challenges we all inevitably face, and see how to deal with them quickly and effectively: finding new business, retaining the business we worked so hard to win and selling more to our existing customers.

Begin by taking the Selling Skills Self-Assessment on page 11. After scoring yourself, look for an area in which you feel you particularly need help. Then read the book through completely. As you progress through the pages, you'll see sections labeled *"Introvert Alert."* That's my way of showing concepts and ideas that are of particular interest and use to those of us who consider ourselves introverts. I've gathered what I consider to be the most useful tips and advice that have helped me throughout my career in these sections and sprinkled them throughout the text.

After your initial reading, I suggest you review those sections that cover areas you marked in the Sales Skills Assessment.

# Contents

# Successful Selling
# For Introverts

# Introduction

My name is Tom Murphy and I am an introvert. I am also a sales and marketing consultant in Portland, Oregon. During the past 25 years I've been a copywriter, advertising assistant, advertising manager, marketing director, vice president of account services and a salesman.

But I assure you I was not born a salesman and never really aspired to be one. As a child, I was not the kid who had the lemonade stand. I was not the kid hustling magazine subscriptions or raffle tickets or whatever fund raising scheme was being promoted that month. No, I was reading Russian history or obscure works by Melville or Twain. I was going to be a great journalist, a foreign correspondent. The idea of selling for a living never crossed my mind.

I graduated from the University of Missouri School of Journalism and then served as an Information Specialist in the Air Force. After my military service I went to work as a marketing specialist for a manufacturer of food store merchandising equipment. Over the next ten years, I created advertising and marketing materials for a number of companies, eventually managing an advertising department for a maker of automobile parts.

Of course, being in marketing and advertising I worked closely with salespeople throughout my career. To me, salespeople were a special breed: hard drinkers (many of them were, but not all), mindless fast-talkers and people with little self-consciousness. They told their customers whatever they wanted to hear and never feared making a cold call or approaching a total stranger

1

to sell them something. That's how I saw salespeople through the first years of my business career. To say the least, I never could see myself selling anything, in person that is. I had a higher calling: to persuade people to buy through indirect means such as advertising, direct mail, brochures and videos.

One day I was offered a job at an advertising agency, where I was told I would be servicing existing accounts. Even then, I didn't see myself as a salesman. There were other professional salespeople that would make the new accounts magically appear. Did I mention I was naïve? I soon discovered that either I became a salesman very quickly or I would become unemployed very quickly. Thus began this introvert's sales career.

Since that day, I have been able to build and expand a base of business at two advertising agencies and developed a loyal following of clients and customers. I have worked with Fortune 500 and 1000 companies, and with small businesses. During this time I was hired and yes, even fired. But, through it all, I was able to gain new accounts and take over existing accounts successfully year after year. Not bad for an introvert.

Over the years I have found thought patterns, actions and attitudes that have been successful in winning new business, increasing business with existing accounts, and retaining customers over time. My desire to share these experiences and insights with others is the reason behind this book. These are real experiences from the real world where most of you live and work.

In writing *Successful Selling for Introverts* I want to first acknowledge that many of us who sell as part of our business are not natural born salespeople; we don't easily envision ourselves influencing others to act in ways that profit us. The selling process to many of us seems very unnatural and unnerving. But, as I have discovered in my career, it doesn't have to be this way. You can be a successful sales person without losing your own personality and without compromising your own beliefs.

I realize many of you are not professional sales people. You may be what I call a "professional who sells" as part of your practice or business. You may be someone who simply "hates to sell" or has said repeatedly, "I'm not a salesman." You may be someone who loves what you do with a passion but can't stomach the fact you have to get out and sell your product to have a viable business. You may be an entrepreneur with a great idea but not a clue on how to sell it to the public. Or you may even be someone who sincerely wants to sell but just doesn't feel you have the techniques to be successful. No matter what circumstances have led you here, you'll find help and assistance throughout *Successful Selling for Introverts*.

Since I first began to sell, I have gained a new respect for selling and salespeople. My initial thoughts were wrong. Selling is tough for everyone, extrovert and introvert alike. Trying to fulfill the wants and desires of your customers is always stressful. If, as an introvert, you are uncomfortable with the concept of selling and doubt your own abilities, the stress is multiplied many times and your opportunities inevitably diminished. Only by approaching selling on your terms and understanding your relationship to other people will you be successful.

One final note. In my sales and marketing consulting practice I face the problems and issues covered in this book on a daily basis. Immediately before beginning my practice, I was a marketing director for a large accounting firm. For the first time in over 10 years I wasn't directly selling and persuading others to buy my services. To my surprise, sales and face-to-face contact with clients had become part of me and I missed it when it I no longer had sales responsibility. That's how transforming my journey has been.

I left that job to become a sales and marketing consultant. I started on day one with no clients or prospects. And of course no income. Today, a few months later, I have accounts and business. Not as much as I will have, but more than I had on the day

I opened my doors. I have been my own research project, using and refining the techniques in this book on a daily basis.

It is my sincere desire that my thoughts and suggestions help you to achieve your dreams and reach your full potential, no matter what type selling you do. In my seminars and consultations I often get direct feedback on the successes that people can achieve with new attitudes and actions brought about with the help of my experiences. Please share your stories by writing me and telling me about your own successes.

Good Selling!

*Tom Murphy*

# Part 1

# The Introvert Salesperson

Selling is one of the most difficult tasks in the business world. Whether selling is your main activity or merely a portion of your overall responsibilities, it can be a real challenge to persuade others to exchange their money for your product or service. To make matters even worse, outside of a marketing course that mentions selling concepts, most of us have never received any formal education in the science of selling.

There is no lack of informal training available however. Books, audiotapes and seminars on selling abound. But I have found that these endeavors rarely address the reader's or listener's fundamental attitude toward sales and selling. They assume, I believe, that salespeople are extroverts for the most part and can easily perform the required actions to be successful. I don't agree.

Perhaps as many as 50% of Americans are introverts. We'll spend some time defining what that term means later, but suffice it to say that the stereotypical salesperson is not an introvert by any means and that sales training books have ignored the possibility of introverts being successful salespeople.

Changes taking place in the business world are increasing the opportunities for introverts to be successful at selling. But sales training has not kept pace. We're going to begin to change that today as you begin reading this book.

# Chapter 1

# Selling Skills
# Self-Assessment

As we set sail on our voyage toward introvert selling success, let's assess your present selling skills by means of what I call a Selling Skills Self-Assessment. Each of the eighteen questions below is designed to probe your feelings toward sales and the selling profession and to explore the skills you have developed so far in your career. Your answers will help to uncover any particular areas in which you have difficulty and direct your attention to the appropriate chapters in this book where you can find help. Take a few minutes to complete the questions and remember to answer as honestly as possible.

Answer "yes" or "no" for each statement below:

1. Selling is an enjoyable part of my business life.
   ☐ yes   ☐ no

2. I see myself as a knowledgeable expert with information and ideas that will help my customers.
   ☐ yes   ☐ no

3. I do at least some research on a company before making a sales contact.
   ☐ yes   ☐ no

4. I never take rejection personally.
   ☐ yes   ☐ no

5. I have a written plan for sales calls and review my performance after each meeting.

☐ yes    ☐ no

6. I know the real benefits my products/services provide for my customers.

☐ yes    ☐ no

7. When I leave a prospect's office or home, I have a reason to contact that person again.

☐ yes    ☐ no

8. I know more than one person at each of my customer locations.

☐ yes    ☐ no

9. I look for other products/services to sell to my existing clients.

☐ yes    ☐ no

10. I know my sales contact's education, hobbies, hometown, family status and pets.

☐ yes    ☐ no

11. I adjust my voice and actions to fit my listener.

☐ yes    ☐ no

12. I can explain my product or service and the benefits it offers in 30 seconds or less.

☐ yes    ☐ no

13. I prepare my voice mail messages in advance in case the person I am calling is not available.

☐ yes    ☐ no

14. I view selling as providing solutions to my customers' problems.

☐ yes    ☐ no

15. I think a sales call on a new prospect is an opportunity to meet a new person and learn about a new company.

☐ yes    ☐ no

16. I have an active personal marketing program in place.

☐ yes ☐ no

17. On a sales call, I listen more than talk.

☐ yes ☐ no

18. I consistently look for signs that a prospect is ready to buy.

☐ yes ☐ no

So how many times did you check "yes"? Here's an easy way to score yourself:

18: Congratulations, you could have helped write this book.

14-17: You're obviously well along on the road to success.

10-12: By picking up this book you are already on your way.

0-9: Read faster!

Before you move ahead, review these eighteen questions one more time. Choose one that really strikes home to you. One that is especially troublesome in your everyday business life. One that, if you changed a no to a yes, would make a significant contribution to your success - today. Then, as you read through the following pages, really focus on the area in which you would like to improve. Make sure you understand the prescription for improvement. By understanding and working on your weak areas will you profit from reading *Successful Selling for Introverts* and achieve the success you so richly deserve.

We'll return to the Selling Skills Self-Assessment at the end of the book to help you gauge your progress.

# Chapter 2

# What Is an Introvert?

Let's start by defining just what this word, "Introvert", means. The dictionary definition is "a person who concentrates on or is directed toward the self." Psychologist Adelaide Bry in her *A Primer of Behavioral Psychology* says, "introverts are thoughtful, peaceable, quiet and considerate of others." She goes on to describe the extrovert, on the other hand, as voluble, outgoing, and persistent.

Don't worry. I'm not going to ask you to take a Myers-Briggs test, the best known indicator of personality type. This is not a psychology textbook. Besides, I think you already have a pretty good idea of where you stand on an introvert-extrovert spectrum. Also, your personality is not static. It most likely varies from day to day, situation to situation.

After all, we're human beings and very few of us fit into nice, little tight compartments. But the more we can understand our own personalities on a day to day basis, the more we can think and acts in ways appropriate to our particular internal makeup. Let's begin by writing down some character traits that you associate with the word "introvert." Write your answers below. Then take a look at my list of introvert traits, which follows.

_____

_____

_____

_____

Here's my list of introvert traits:

- Inwardly directed
- Quiet
- Thinks about and prepares for actions and decisions
- Studious
- Smart
- Tempered
- Detail Oriented
- Less expressive
- Non-confrontational
- Speaks more slowly
- Likes personal space
- Self Contained
- Concentrates on depth and theory
- Non-aggressive
- Considerate
- Better at one-to-one relationships

Do you agree with my list? How does it compare to your list?

Do any of these describe you? Write down the introvert traits that describe you, at least some of the time. Remember, very few of us are complete introverts or extroverts. Most of us have some traits from both extremes.

Sometimes I am: _____

_____

_____

_____

Now let's look at extroverts. What character traits do you usually associate with the word "extrovert?"

_____

_____

_____

_____

Again, here's my list:

- Enjoy action

- Act quickly

- Welcome variety

- Impatient with slower tasks

- Interested in achieving goal and results

- People-oriented

- Expressive

- Sociable

- Make premature decisions based on enthusiasm

- Comfortable in a crowd

How does it compare to your list? Do you have any characteristics of an extrovert?

Write down any extrovert traits that apply to you, if any, at least some of the time.

_____

_____

_____

We'll come back to these shortly.

Perhaps the best way to explain the basic difference between an introvert and an extrovert is that introverts lose energy when they are with people and recharge when they are alone. Extroverts, on the other hand, lose energy when they are alone and recharge when they are with people.

Let me make a point here. I don't for one moment mean to imply or suggest in any way that introversion is superior to extroversion or vice versa. Quite the contrary. Like the color of our skin or hair, our predilection toward introversion or extroversion is, I believe, inherited through our genes and reinforced by our experiences as we mature. But, unlike those two examples, an individual can change his or her orientation through choice and hard work. It isn't easy, but it can be done. It is my contention, however, that you do not have to change your personality to that of an extrovert to be successful in sales. You simply have to know yourself and act in harmony with your personality.

Don't confuse introversion with shyness. They are not the same. In fact, many introverts are not shy and do not recoil from social contact. They simply prefer to be quieter and more cerebral the majority of the time, following an internal compass rather than an external one. Conversely, there are numerous examples of shy extroverts. For instance, many actors and actresses are certainly extroverts in that they crave the attention and adoration of others. However, in private, outside the controlled "role" they are playing, they are shy and almost reclusive.

Shyness is a condition that can be detrimental to our lives if it becomes obsessive and can be improved through practice and exposure to uncomfortable social situations. Introversion is a character or personality trait that doesn't need to be changed. It needs to be recognized and used effectively.

But enough of these textbook-type definitions. We can find our own real world examples of what constitutes an introvert. So with apologies to Jeff Foxworthy and his "You Know You're a Redneck When..." comedy routines, you know you're an introvert when...

• You listen more than you talk.

• You enjoy reading a book more than going to a party.

• You spend more time reading or working at your computer than visiting friends.

• You have a few really close friends rather than a large group of acquaintances.

• You appreciate having time to yourself.

• You usually spend time thinking before you act.

For most of us, the title introvert simply means we are more comfortable with ourselves than with others and we are not "people persons." Our introversion is a personality type that results in some life and career choices but doesn't restrict our happiness or ability to function in business or society.

Historically, introversion has been associated more with the professions and with artists; anyone steeped in knowledge or creativity gained through rigorous study. Lawyers, architects, accountants, artists, and writers usually come to mind when the word introvert is used. Extroversion has been associated with sales, marketing and business management professions. While these are the stereotypes associated with personality types, they are not without exceptions. Some of the most introverted people I have ever known were very successful in the advertising agency business and some of the most extroverted people I've known were accountants.

### Summary

Understanding yourself is a prerequisite for success in any endeavor. And no matter how many definitions are offered to explain our personalities, we are all unique combinations of personality traits that can confound the most learned of psychologists. The main point of this introductory chapter on introversion is to help recognize your introvert traits and begin to understand that they are not insurmountable obstacles to selling success. In fact, in the next chapter we will see how your introvert traits just might be the key to your ultimate success.

# Chapter 3

# Introversion's Positive Side

Let's take another look at the list of introvert traits:

- Inwardly directed
- Quiet
- Thinks about and prepares for actions and decisions
- Studious
- Smart
- Tempered
- Detail Oriented
- Less expressive
- Non-confrontational
- Speaks more slowly
- Likes personal space
- Self Contained
- Concentrates on depth and theory
- Non-aggressive
- Considerate
- Better at one-to-one relationships

As a typical introvert, you might look at this list of introvert

- Non-aggressive

- Considerate

- Better at one-to-one relationships

These traits may make you a good accountant, lawyer, architect or other professional but they are not characteristics you usually link with people who are successful in sales. So it's no wonder that, as an introvert, you doubt your sales abilities. These doubts can inhibit you from visualizing yourself as being successful in selling and taking the actions necessary to sell your services or products on a consistent basis. You must address and overcome these doubts if you are to achieve the success you desire.

To do so, let's take another look at your introvert character traits. As I wrote in the introduction to this book, much of my background is in the advertising business, where the main task is to communicate product (that's you in this instance) or service features in the form of benefits to customers. With that purpose in mind, let's revisit your introvert character traits again, this time from a customer's perspective.

Here's an example to help you get started.

## Quiet = Great listener

The most successful salespeople are great listeners. You can't be a great listener if you are talking most of the time. At its basic level, selling is listening to a person's needs and then offering a solution that the buyer perceives as valuable enough to exchange money for. It's that simple. And as we'll learn, changes in the selling are placing an even greater emphasis on superior listening skills.

According to a well-known sales training axiom, successful salespeople spend 70% of their selling time listening to customers and prospects. Tell me, who do you think is the better listener, the quiet introvert or the expressive extrovert? We all know the born-salesperson type who doesn't shut up. When they're speaking, they can't be listening to their clients and prospects, finding needs to be fulfilled.

Now try this exercise yourself. Write down your list of introvert characteristics and come up with a customer-friendly perspective on each. Reflect on your personality characteristics from your customer's viewpoint. Try to see how they see you. Be positive.

| Introvert Characteristic | | Customer Perspective |
|---|---|---|
| _____ | = | _____ |
| _____ | = | _____ |
| _____ | = | _____ |
| _____ | = | _____ |
| _____ | = | _____ |

Here are some of these new customer-focused perspectives on characteristics from my list:

### Inwardly directed =Focused

You know what you want to do and why. You are not susceptible to being whatever the customer wants. You are customer focused but follow your own internal compass. There is substance to you. Obviously, the more your business relies upon specialized knowledge, the more important this particular attribute becomes. Don't be afraid to show that you are serious about your profession or business. Your customers will appreciate you and come to rely upon your expertise.

### Studious = knowledgeable

The day of the sales person armed with a smile, a shoe shine and a price list are dead. In today's ever more information-based economy, knowledge is an indispensable part of a sales person's success. The information you possess about your service or product makes you valuable to your customers and prospects. The more information you have, the more valuable you are. This would seem to be self-evident, but it continually amazes me how often I'm accosted by salespeople with little more than a rudimentary knowledge of their product. Separate yourself from the fast-talking sales types known more for their pitch than their product knowledge. Show yourself to be "the fount of all knowledge" in your chosen area. Make sure your customers know and appreciate your abilities.

$$\frac{\text{Think about and prepare for actions and decisions}}{} = \text{respected, taken seriously}$$

This is a real advantage of being an introvert. As people come to appreciate you and understand that you don't "run off at the mouth", they will respect your counsel and seek out your opinion. An introvert doesn't "tell them what they want to hear." A successful introvert salesperson listens closely, thinks about solutions to the customer's problems and then offers considered opinions. As an added bonus, the value of the introvert sales person increases as the value of the product or service being sold increases.

## Non-aggressive = non-threatening

The perception of introverts as non-aggressive is perhaps the greatest disservice done to us. Because much of the introvert's selling consists of preparation and planning, others may perceive us as not having "the fire in the belly" or the aggressiveness needed to be successful. But again, take a look at the situation from the customer's viewpoint. To the customer, the aggressiveness desired by sales managers is really a negative. Who wants to be pounced upon and pursued like wild game? This "in-your-face" school of selling is increasingly confined to consumer in-home selling and automobile dealers. The salesperson who is not instantly typecast as an aggressive salesperson can build trust and appreciation more easily than the aggressive "in your face" type.

Sales training guru Tom Hopkins calls it "Low Profile Selling." Others call it relationship selling. What it is is a cease-fire in the war of seller vs. buyer. The old paradigm was to trick or force they buyer into a hasty decision, then make a quick retreat to the next mark. In-home sales were notorious for this type approach. It still goes on today but it is fading. And quite frankly, I would advise anyone who identifies with introvert character traits to avoid this type selling.

The new paradigm is creating a win-win relationship with your customers. Go for additional sales, for referrals, for a relationship. A great example of someone who built this type relationship many years ago is Joe Girard, at one time the world's greatest car salesman. In his book, *How to Sell Anything to Anybody,* Girard concentrates on giving real value to his customers and working them for repeat and referral sales. If he can do it in car sales, it can be done anywhere. If only every car salesperson was like Joe.

## Considerate = well-liked

It is often said that people buy from people they like. In my experience that is mostly true. Unless you have a product that turns water into gold, you need to be aware of your customer's feelings and try to make them like you. The introvert trait of being considerate of others can go along way to building people's positive reactions to you. But don't be too nice. That can get you into trouble back at your office and, alas, you can be susceptible to being taken advantage of by your customers.

## Better at one-to-one relationships = focused on customer

Rather than flitting from one "conquest" to another, you really care about your customers and want to make sure they have been satisfied. People sell to people and although extroverts seem to be more people-oriented, there is no law that says introverts can't be just as people-oriented, only with fewer people. You can make your customers those special people.

After going through your personal "new perspective" review, you should be able to say something like this: "I'm a person with great self-knowledge, a keen listening ear, who is respected and taken seriously, has great product knowledge, is perceived as non-threatening and is well-liked."

Isn't that a much more powerful self-image? Once you see yourself in this positive light and understand just how much you have to offer, then you can concentrate on how best to convey your unique personality to your clients and prospects.

## Do It Your Way

Two of my great sports interests are baseball and running. In both, success depends upon the athlete making the best use of his abilities and adopting styles appropriate for him or her. Former Minnesota Twins player Rod Carew holds many of the all-time hitting records. Year after year he hit .350 plus, and yet, his hitting stance broke every rule taught in organized baseball from little league to the majors. But Carew's stance worked for him and his success speaks for itself.

In marathon running, Alberto Salazar is one of the all-time greats. He won the New York Marathon, the Boston Marathon and has now even been successful in ultramarathons. I could go on and on about how his style of running is not fluid and breaks all the rules taught to young runners. But again, Salazar was successful because he found his own style and built a great career on it.

You can do the same. Know your unique selling style and appreciate your abilities by making the most of them. Work relentlessly at perfecting your performance and you will find sales success.

## Summary

Did you do the exercises in this chapter? Can you see yourself in a different light? Positioning is a term that is used in marketing products and services, but it should also apply to marketing yourself, both to others and to you. I'm convinced that with a little positive thought, each one of us can position ourselves in a way that is helpful to our selling endeavors and to gaining a positive self-image of ourselves whether in selling activities or any other part of our lives.

# Part 2

# Six Pillars of Introvert Sales Success

Now that you can see yourself and your unique person ality in a positive light, let's look at how you can turn your new positive attitude into sales success. What follows are what I call *Six Pillars of Introvert Sales Success*, each one a critical element in building selling skill. While the six elements are necessary for introverts and extroverts alike, I will emphasize how each of these, when applied correctly, can work to the advantage of the more introverted of us. The Six Pillars of Introvert Sales Success are:

- Attitude
- Product/Service Knowledge
- Customer Knowledge
- The Ability to Build Personal Relationships
- Flexibility
- Persistence

# Chapter 4

# Pillar #1: Attitude

As with most things in life, successful selling begins with a positive attitude toward yourself and toward your selling activities. Because introverts are so inwardly directed, it is very difficult for introverts to be untrue to themselves. What you see on the outside is usually what is on the inside. So it is of utmost importance that we feel good to ward ourselves and how we conduct our business lives.

We've already discussed how we can look at our introvert personality traits in a new, positive manner that focuses on the benefits we as individuals can offer our customers. Armed with this new self-respect toward ourselves, we can now look at how society's prejudices toward selling may affect our attitudes and keep us from finding the success we could otherwise enjoy.

Think for a moment of how a change in your attitude could affect your business life. Obviously, if you could sell more of your product or service you would make more money and enjoy greater success. In addition, it is often said that someone who can sell is virtually unemployment proof. There will always be a need for those who can turn their commitment to customer satisfaction and problem solving into sales. The rewards are certainly there for those who can sell.

## Fear and Loathing of Sales

One of the major obstacles to selling success, especially among professionals, is a negative perception of selling and salespeople. Many people equate selling with a "Music Man" mentality, where a slick, fast talker takes advantage of others, selling them what they don't need and wouldn't otherwise buy. They picture selling as a zero sum game where someone wins and someone loses. As a consequence of these beliefs, they prefer not to see themselves as salespeople and they hesitate to take the type actions that create sales success.

The sales profession doesn't help its self image either. Look at the vocabulary often used in sales training: target, be aggressive, overcome objections, close, tactics. Sales is talked about in terms of warfare and battlefields. The crafty salesperson against the dupe. Are they selling us something or trying to strong-arm us? Is this business or war?

I recently received a flyer promoting a sales training program that I can only say is representative of the stereotypical sales type. Just a few words of copy will give you an idea of the mindset behind this training:

"Break through the resistance...orchestrate a controlled closing that cinches the sale...strike while the iron is hot...conquer a prospect's fear of committal...create a closing plan that works for you."

Not one word about fulfilling a need or creating a win-win situation. To me the tactics described are more appropriate for a carnival game operator than a professional salesperson and even more inappropriate for a professional person selling his or her services.

Popular culture certainly doesn't build an appreciation for sales either. Fox's *Married With Children* had shoe salesmen Al Bundy as the ultimate buffoon, hating his career and his customers. For those of you a few years older or addicted to reruns, *WKRP in Cincinnati* had the infamous Herb Tarleck selling time on the station, wearing garish outfits that would make a used car salesman blush. Mamet's *Glengary Crossing* featured foul-mouthed real estate salesmen clawing at each other and chewing up the weak and old. And of course, Miller's *Death of a Salesman* gave pitiful Willy Loman to the ages. Plus, don't forget the easy-to-satirize late night used car salesman hawking a low mileage beauty.

Americans seem to be buying this negative image of salespeople. The 1997 Gallup Poll asked random samples of people to rank 26 professions according to the amount of trust they felt in each. At the bottom was the much-aligned car salesperson, slightly ahead of the insurance salesman. Even Congress ranked higher in public trust. "Mommas Don't Let Your Babies Grow Up to Be Salespeople" seems to be America's favorite refrain.

Even the sales industry itself seems to buy into this negative characterization. The September 1997 issue of Sales and Marketing Management which should know better, shows a stereotypical, con-man type used car salesman in their story about how to lease a car.

Take a look at television to see how we view the professions. You have the dedicated doctors trying to save lives. The socially sensitive lawyer defends the poor. Newspaper and magazine writers live glamorous lives exposing society's hidden truths. Factory workers nobly put in their long hours. And of course there is the unending parade of police, rescue squads, firefighters, private detectives and other defenders of our civility shown in dramatic situations.

I'll give you a dramatic situation. How about making a presentation for a million dollar program that's going to give you enough commission to buy that new car you need because the Gremlin is going to break down in the middle of the highway on your way to your next sales call. I'd like to see that on television.

With no positive role models, is it any wonder that, as a society, we think salespeople are untrustworthy and negative.

Take a moment to think about a positive role model of a salesperson in popular culture. Then write that character's name on the lines below. What makes them a positive role model?

Character _____

Positive Character Traits _____

_____

_____

Now write down the name of a positive role model of a salesperson, or person with some sales responsibilities in your own life. Do you ever see these type people portrayed in the media?

Person _____

Character Traits _____

_____

_____

The sales training industry has been slow to recognize the changes in the selling environment I outline in Chapter 10. Instead of focusing on how to satisfy the consumer, they have focused on how to cope with the pressures brought on by the constant combat they see as selling. They have tons of motivation tapes and chants that kept you plugging away at the prospects armed with your 15 different closes and 23 ways to overcome objections.

Sales gurus advise that if you just make 100 sales calls a day reading your script, you'll get two replies. If you need four replies, make 200 calls. They never discuss the 196 out of 200 people called that are turned off to salespeople by the call. They never discuss the negative self-image such self-abuse gives to many salespeople.

I'll admit, some of this type training works. It must. A lot of people sell a lot of products. It may have worked for you. But in the vast majority of cases, sales training has not addressed the fundamental issues of what selling is and what it means to be a salesperson. As a result, many capable people simply avoid any association with sales and allow others to do the selling and reap the rewards.

## I'm Not a Salesman, I'm an Account Executive

One of the most interesting people I ever had the fortune to meet was Wally Armbruster. He was the creative director for D'Arcy Maisus Benton and Bowles advertising in St. Louis. You probably never heard of Wally but you've certainly heard or seen his work. He was responsible for many of the famous jingles and slogans associated with Budweiser Beer such as "When You Say Bud, you've said it all." Wally was one of the most direct, clear thinkers of all time and he helped build brands such as Bud, Ralston Purina, Red Lobster and Southwestern Bell Telephone.

Advertising was Wally's day job. But his real passion was Salesmanship. Wally wrote a great little book entitled, *Where Have All the Salesmen Gone?* I recommend it highly. It was his contention that, although we all are salespeople of one sort or another, we aren't comfortable with the identification and hide it under a masquerade of titles such as Customer Service Representative, Account Manager, Account Executive, Director of Sales and Marketing, Manufacturer's Representative, Product Manager and so on. But, no matter what our business card reads, we are all salespeople, like it or not.

We're all salespeople in that we persuade others to act in a way that we define as good or appropriate. Don't teachers sell students on the benefit of learning? Don't religious leaders persuade congregations to act righteously and support their ministry financially? And even in our own families, don't we persuade our children to act responsibly and contribute to society?

## The Real Meaning of Selling

So let's drop the pretense. We all sell, some more overtly than others. Some of us are professional salespeople. Some are professionals who sell as part of a practice. Either way, we all engage in selling. And that's not bad. Even if society portrays salespeople negatively, we don't have to accept that characterization. Get rid of these negative thoughts and concentrate on the real positive meaning of sales.

### Selling is fulfilling a customer's needs or desires with a product or service.

It's that simple. It's not a fight to outsmart a stupid consumer. It's not a game pitting you against the buyer. It is fulfilling a need. The sales process is finding someone whose needs can possibly be met by your product or service; examining those needs in detail; explaining how your product or service best meets those needs; showing how the buyers investment is commensurate with the benefit they will receive from your product or service; and persuading the buyer that your solution to their problem is the best solution. And one thing more – asking the buyer to take action and make a commitment by purchasing your product or service.

Does that sound so bad? Well that is sales, pure and simple.

Get rid of the negative baggage. Selling is a noble profession. Professionals can and indeed must sell their services and expertise. It's not degrading or unprofessional. Today's business environment demands sales skills.

Notice, I didn't say it was easy. Sometimes you have to uncover a buyer's true needs. Sometimes they don't recognize your product's benefits as readily as you do. But the bottom line is that there is nothing inherently wrong or immoral with selling and persuasion. Selling is a prerequisite for a free market economy such as ours. So until the rules change, being able to sell your product or service is a prerequisite for success.

### Attitude Toward Your Customer

Hand in hand with your attitude toward the act of selling is your attitude toward your customer. It's a sad fact that some salespeople do view their customers and prospects as merely the pathway to commission checks. But in today's world of increased buyer wariness, this exploitative attitude can be a real detriment to your long-term sales success and is no substitute for a dedication to fulfilling your customers' needs. As I said above, those of us who are introverted have a difficult time being something we are not and, if we have a negative attitude toward our clients, it will show eventually.

In a professional services situation, or in selling any product or service where on-going sales and contact is required, such an attitude will sooner or later surface to the detriment of the relationship. Focusing on commissions and short term advantage is clearly the domain of the fast-talking sales stereotype of the past.

By contrast, focusing on the customer and filling needs is the surest way to fat commission checks today and tomorrow. Remember, we said people buy from people they like. When you show that you care about them and want to help them in some way, people will like you. When you enter a business relationship with this attitude you are on the road to long-lasting success from on-going sales to existing customers and new business from enthusiastic referrals.

## Be Yourself

Once you have examined your unique set of personality characteristics and looked at them in a customer-friendly way, make sure you convey your true self to your customers and prospects. Growing up in the 60's, I thought there was no worse pejorative than calling someone a "phony." It meant that you were not true to yourself, were manipulative of others and certainly not likable. Obviously, that's not what we want to convey to our customers and prospects.

When I first started working in an advertising agency I had the opportunity to see phoniness in action. I was teamed with a man who had been a great success in advertising in Chicago but over the preceding years had steadily declined from working at world class agencies to toiling away at a smaller agency in St. Louis. He was a classic introvert. But he didn't know it. He knew advertising inside and out. He was a pilot and a student of history. He read sales training books. He knew the openings, the closes, and the icebreakers. But he didn't know himself.

Preparing for a sales call, he would chain smoke and shake, almost uncontrollably. If it were a social occasion, he would need a couple of martinis before wading into the crowd. Driving with me to a presentation for a prospective client, he would discuss every move like a military campaign, telling me when to interject a comment, when to bring up our agency's group of experienced professionals and when to leave the talking to him.

What he didn't do was think of the prospect's needs and expectations. He didn't put himself in the prospect's chair. He was all style and little substance. Instead of sharing his knowledge and showing how he (we) could benefit the prospect, he focused on sales tactics more appropriate for selling replacement windows to gullible homeowners.

During the actual presentation, he was stiff, haughty, and formal with an air of condescension. With existing clients, he was the same way. It was a shame, because he was a very knowledgeable person and, with a different outlook, could have made great contributions to his clients and our agency.

But, as you can guess, he didn't attract new business and saw a steady erosion of his existing clients. The message is: Be yourself. All the tactics in the world won't work for you if people can't see the real you beneath the tactics. My mentor would have been less nervous had he concentrated on our prospects needs and desires rather than his own tactics. His pre-meeting difficulties were signals that he wasn't being true to himself. He couldn't help but betray his inner conflict to the world.

To illustrate how potent a true, warm personality can be, let me tell you about a printing salesman I had the good fortune to meet. I was new to buying printing but had quite a large number of four-color multi-page printing projects under my control. As you can imagine, printing salesmen were all over me; good ones, bad ones and most somewhere in between. The man who stood out and received the majority of my business was Bob Lahlein.

Bob was a quiet man. He spoke softly. He didn't belong to a country club and never had a skybox to baseball or football games. He never slapped me on the back or told me a joke. If he ever closed on me I never felt it. And while he always dressed appropriately, he never overdressed or tried to impress me with his car. Lunch with Bob was more likely to be Denny's than a trendy bar.

But what he did do was take care of every printing need I ever had. He knew printing inside and out. Oftentimes he would tell me that his firm could not compete on a particular job, but that he knew someone who could. I never was left in the dark about when my printing jobs would be delivered. And when there was, as there is in any business relationship, a problem or a concern, he took total responsibility and resolved problems quickly.

As you might expect, Bob was successful not only with me, but also with many other loyal clients. It is easy to see why. Look at him from my new customer-focused perspective. He was not quiet; he was a good listener. He was not only studious, but his product knowledge outshone any of his competitors. And I can tell you that his dedication to detail was appreciated.

Now there may be a skeptic out there. Of course, handling accounts can be the introvert's domain, but what about new business? You have to be aggressive to get new business.

Of course you do. But there are different ways to be aggressive. Bob was consistently the top salesman for his printing company and I don't think he ever made a cold call. That's because he had a sales force of hundreds of customers like me singing his praises and building his business. He was aggressive at being good.

Was Bob an introvert? Yes. Was he successful? He was very successful by being himself.

## Summary

Your attitude toward your selling efforts is obviously very important and a key to your success. From my seminars, I find that very few people who sell as part of their profession will overtly admit a negative attitude toward selling. But as we discuss their attitudes in depth it is not surprising to hear words like "have to sell" or "become a peddler" creep into their vocabulary. This tells me that many of my attendees harbor deep antipathies toward seeing themselves as salespeople. These feelings, though kept below the surface, can be significant barriers toward ultimate success because they keep you from learning to enjoy selling and continuing to sell, even when you reach a certain level of success. Before you proceed, take a moment to reflect on your true thoughts about selling. Don't let a negative attitude hold you back from real success.

# Chapter 5

# Pillar #2:
# Customer Knowledge

Information about your prospective customer is an important weapon in the introvert's successful selling arsenal. Exhibiting a grasp of important information about your target company immediately sets you apart from the vast majority of salespeople. It positions you as a serious, customer-focused sales professional who cares enough to invest time and effort to know basic facts about your prospect. When you're recognized as someone special, you'll find those walls crumble and lines of communication open.

In addition, the more you know about a prospective customer and his or her company, the easier it is to initiate conversations and small talk. You are not restricted to mentioning the golf award on the wall if you can comment on the nice rise in the company stock price over the last month.

It always amazes me how many salespeople do little or nothing to become acquainted with prospect companies before attempting to sell them something. I've had salespeople literally sit down and say, "tell me a little bit about your company." That's not a very good first impression. Most of us are too busy to educate salespeople on the basics of our companies.

Don't be like the young salesman who called on me when I was Director of Marketing for an office of a large, international

accounting firm. He came to see me to solicit the firm's partici-
pation in sponsoring a three-on-three street basketball tournament. He sat down and immediately began to tell me all the
wonderful facts about the tournament; the number of participants, the expected attendance and media coverage. It would be
a great opportunity to build awareness of my firm.

I asked him if he knew to whom we targeted our accounting
and tax services. Of course, he had no idea. I went on to tell
him that middle-aged CEO's and CFO's of public companies
with annual revenue of $20 million or more were unlikely to be
fans of three-on-three basketball. He left without a sponsor.

Here's a list of the basic information you should have for
each prospective company or individual customer before attempting to sell to them.

## Customer Knowledge Checklist

**Business-to-Business Sales**

- ☐ Organizational Structure
- ☐ Products and Markets
- ☐ Broad goals and objectives
- ☐ Company history
- ☐ Strengths and weaknesses
- ☐ How my product adds value to clients product
- ☐ Stock price, if public
- ☐ Ownership, if private
- ☐ Banks, lawyers, accountants
- ☐ Unionization of sales force (where applicable)
- ☐ Marketing organization

**Consumer Sales**

- ☐ Family Makeup

☐ Jobs

☐ Drivers (status, money, family, etc.)

☐ How they will use my product/service

☐ Attitude toward risk

## Where to Find Company Information

So how do you find information on prospective customers? It's easier than you think. Here are just a few resources:

*The newspaper.* The business section is full of information you can use in your selling endeavors. Executive appointments, quarterly earnings, new construction and other information appear daily. Spend more time reading the business section and less reading sports. Cut out and save articles you want to keep and start a file folder full of facts on companies you would like to have as customers.

*Your local library.* Did you know most libraries have your local newspaper archived on microfiche or CD-ROM? Sit at the terminal, type in the company you want to track and in just a few seconds you'll have every reference to a company from the newspaper over the last one to five years. You can do it in the time it takes to get a cup of coffee. The reference section has plenty of other resources you can use, such as directories and databases. Tell the reference librarian what you're looking for and he or she will point you in the right direction

*The Internet.* Just about every public company has a web site with all the information you need. Larger private companies have sites also. It's incredible what you can find in just a few minutes surfing the web. The American Business Journal group of local business papers has on-line versions that you can search for information about particular companies and industries. Just type "Business Journal" in any search engine and you will be able to access any and all of the local papers. If you can't access the web at home, try the library. Most now have access.

*Stock.* If you have a public target and want to stay on top of its operations, buy a share of stock. You'll get annual and quarterly reports automatically.

*The lobby.* If you haven't done any homework before the time you meet with your prospective buyer, the lobby is your resource of last resort. Plan on being at least ten minutes early for your appointment. In the lobby you can usually find magazines of interest to the company. Many of the magazines may even carry ads from your prospect company. Use the index of advertisers in the back of most trade magazines to quickly see if your prospect is among the advertisers.

Many companies have a product display in the lobby. You can look it over and think of a question or comment that shows you have at least some knowledge of the company. You'll find product literature in many lobbies also. Take the opportunity to read it before your appointment and then take it along when you leave.

If you are selling to consumers, you usually won't have much information before making your sales call. However, during your initial minutes of meeting with a prospective customer you can turn small talk into information gathering. Find out the family makeup, jobs, how they intend to use your product or service and what drives their purchase: status, money, family, community. You'll then be better able to tailor your presentation to their particular areas of interest. Never assume you can know the answers by simply looking around the prospects' home. You might be wrong.

## After You Have the Business

Just because you are successful at getting business from a prospect doesn't mean you can discontinue your research efforts. If anything, you should intensify your dedication to knowing as much as possible about your customer or client. You'll have more opportunities to show your knowledge, so you'll need to stay current.

Of course the depth of your knowledge will vary depending on the product or service you are supplying. For instance, when I was an advertising account executive, I needed to have a great depth of knowledge about my clients' products and markets. On the other hand, if you are selling office supplies you probably don't need to know as much about your customers. But you should still stay abreast of the latest information and show you are part of the company team. Remember that the whole idea is to be perceived as a team member. The worst thing a client ever called me was a "vendor." I hate that word and you should too. To me, it denotes a less than full partnership between the buyer and seller. It also seems condescending.

As an account executive I always read my clients' industry publications. Over the years, I've read everything from *WasteWater Journal* to *Dairy Cow Management* to *Modern Materials Handling*. Although my family thought I was a little crazy when they saw my evening reading, my clients appreciated the occasional clipped article or piece of competitive information I was able to glean from my eclectic sources.

If you are a major supplier to a company, you might also consider visiting their industry trade shows. You'll find they are wonderful opportunities to show your dedication to your clients and, you might even pick up leads on other prospects in that general industry. But don't go at the peak attendance hours. The people you'll want to talk to are busy then. Try late in the afternoon or first thing the second or third day of a trade show. And if you want to get some market intelligence, stay for the last few hours of the show. The salespeople on the floor are bored and anxious to talk to anyone with a smile. You'll find the sales guy from Ottawa will be more than happy to discuss his company, if for no other reason than to pass the time as he waits for the show to end.

---

### Introvert Alert

At first glance, a trade show would seem to be an introvert's worst nightmare. Thousand of people, crowded into small aisles, all trying to sell something to someone. But trade shows are a great way to gather information about your clients and their competitors plus meet other prospects for your product or services. The trick is to pick the right time to walk the show floor. During the shows peak hours you can get caught up in the mass of people. Try late in the day when the crowds have thinned out. That's when the folks manning the booths have more time to talk and discuss their products in depth. Just walk into the booth and look at an item of interest. You'll be approached by someone and into a conversation quickly and easily.

---

Do you read your customer's sales literature? If you want to understand their markets and products, it's a great way to increase your knowledge. And it's easy to get. Just ask. If you sell a part for a piece of machinery, have you ever seen that machine in operation? You should. Never let an opportunity to further your knowledge about a customer pass without taking advantage of it.

## Taking Over an Existing Account

In theory this should be your easiest assignment. The ice has been broken. The customer knows your company and is probably satisfied. You only need to keep things moving and show up. However, that mindset couldn't be further from the truth. In fact, taking over an existing account can be the most challenging type of sales assignment.

Both as an advertising manager and as an account executive in an agency, I was continually bombarded with new sales reps for trade publications that were soliciting advertising. For some reason, turnover among magazine and newspaper space salespeople is extremely high. I always cringed when I received a call that began..."Mr. Murphy, this is Angela, your new sales rep for Modern Motors. I'd like to meet with you to learn all about your company (or client)."

It was very unusual for a new sales rep to betray even the slightest knowledge of my company or client. Didn't they at least talk to their predecessor or read a file that detailed our history with them? Unfortunately, most of the time they had not one iota of information.

By not showing any knowledge about me or my company, the new salesperson lost all the advantages of incumbency. What if my new sales rep had introduced herself like this: "Mr. Murphy, this is Angela, your new sales rep for Modern Motors. I see you ran five ads with us last year and I hope you plan to continue this year. Do you still do your planning in October? I'd like to meet with you at your earliest convenience to bring you up to date on our plans for next year."

Now that's using the power of incumbency.

The secret is to treat your new account exactly as if it were completely new business. Do your homework. Find out as much as you can about the company. When you meet your contacts, show them you have done your homework. You want them to feel comfortable. I can tell you that, from the buyer's point of view, a change in the sales person working on your account is greeted with trepidation and concern. Your competitors will be looking to take advantage of the situation.

In the advertising business, a change of account executives is like a drop of blood in a shark-infested ocean. Other agencies go into a feeding frenzy knowing that the account is most vulnerable at that time. My experience in public accounting was similar and I'm willing to bet that whatever industry you are in, a change of salespeople is a very vulnerable time for a company.

The successful introvert sales person welcomes the opportunity to take over an existing account. The initial courting to obtain the account is over and most likely the client only wants to know that nothing will change. Your first objective should be to soothe the customer's nerves by show your expertise and concern as soon as possible. Build trust by being serious and focused on providing even better service to the client. Once the initial period of concern is over, the client will transfer his or her loyalties to you and the account will be yours.

**Talk with your customer's distributors and salespeople.**

Get permission first, but make it a part of your research efforts to talk with your customer's front-line salespeople. That's the way to get to the bottom of issues, the way to find out what is really going on. In my agency days, we never made a presentation to a prospect without first talking to people that sold the product or service. They loved being included in our research and they always had an opinion to share. But don't just use this tactic at the beginning of a relationship. Use it to keep abreast of what is happening at the customer company and in the industry. Then use the information to better serve your client.

## Summary

Make a commitment, starting today, to always have at least some basic information about your prospect before you make a sales call. As I said, you'll immediately go to the front of the sales class due to the fact so many salespeople neglect this simple rule. Once you have the business, expand your knowledge base continually, using all the sources listed above. Make yourself a team member, not a vendor, and you'll reap the sales rewards over time.

# Chapter 6

# Pillar #3:
# Product Knowledge

Every salesperson must know their product or service. At first, this may seem self-evident. But what I mean is superior knowledge, above and beyond the expected. Nothing can kill a sale more quickly than showing a lack of understanding or knowledge about your own product. It has always amazed me when salespeople have called on me armed with nothing more than rudimentary knowledge of what they were selling. I've had salespeople who were unable to answer simple questions and seemed to be totally unaware of competitor offerings.

Here's a handy checklist to follow when assessing your own level of knowledge:

### Product Knowledge Checklist

☐ What makes your product special?
This is the most important piece of information you possess. What sets your product or service apart from your competitors? Make sure this is expressed in the form of a benefit to the customer. Don't leave your office until you can quickly and clearly answer this question. Don't leave your prospect's office until he or she can answer this question.

☐ Features and Benefits
Be sure you know the difference between a feature and a ben-

efit. Never mention one without the other. Make sure you completely understand your brochures and flyers, so that you will not be embarrassed in front of your prospect.

### ❒ Legal Requirements
The use of many products or services is covered by legal and regulatory restraints. Don't assume your customer knows all of these. Review any legal questions with proper counsel or management before speaking to customers.

### ❒ Customer's application
Make sure you understand how your customer will use your product or service. You should already have this information in order to know how to fulfill your prospect's needs, but having an in-depth knowledge from your customer's perspective will build your stature during the sales call.

### ❒ Customization options
No one wants off the shelf today. Know what options are available to your customers without having to check with the home office and you will build extra trust with your customers.

### ❒ Similar satisfied customers
Most people buying products or services for their companies tend to be very conservative. They want to know who has made a commitment to you and what experience they have had with you. Be ready. I often counsel my clients to have printed flyers that highlight other customers in a problem/solution type format that is easy to use and leave with the prospect after the sales call. If possible, provide names and phone numbers of satisfied customers and invite the prospect to call them. This can be a powerful way to move the prospect to a commitment.

### ❒ Quality Guarantees
This also serves to calm the usual nervousness that accompanies making a commitment to a product or service. Have it in writing and in simple language that explains what you will and will

not do. Most large companies have these, but small companies need them just as well.

❏ Pricing and justification

By justification I mean sell value, not just price. An ocean-side hotel operator I recently spoke with understood this concept all too well. His greatest concern was how his staff answered the question, "How much are your rooms?" Being a remarkably good marketer for a small hotel owner, he knew that he didn't sell rooms. He sold a lodging experience that included the ocean view, his pool, his exercise room and his dining room. Giving someone a price for a room was a no-win situation for him. The caller could only judge the relative cost of hotel rooms, not of lodging experiences. The hotel owner instructed all his employees to tell any caller of the hotel's amenities before mentioning any price. He even told them to end by saying, "and all of this at only $XX per night." A great marketer.

❏ Competition

I've always found gathering competitive intelligence to be one of the most difficult yet rewarding aspects of selling. The more you know about your competitors the better you can sell. Don't disparage your competitors, but do be aware of their shortcomings. Then emphasize those areas in which you and your company excel. In my marketing communications practice I know that most small companies offer only one aspect of communications such as public relations, writing or graphic design. On the other hand, large advertising agencies offer a variety of services but also have an enormous amount of overhead to cover. I therefore try to offer a multitude of services but on a "virtual" agency basis that avoids the overhead and high costs of agencies. I continually emphasize this point in my sales presentations and flyers.

❏ Flaws (don't tell, just know)

Very few things in this life are perfect. Most likely your product or service is not one of the few. So, in order not to be surprised by a prospect, you should take a realistic view of your offering and know what potential liabilities and problems you may have. Develop an honest answer to this problem and be ready to use it in the unlikely event it comes up. Be a Boy Scout. *Be Prepared.*

❐ Delivery times and methods

This may not always be possible but should be your goal – to know when you can deliver a product or begin a service. After making a commitment to you, your new customer will be anxious to see the tangible results of his or her decision. If you have to be vague about delivery schedules, you run the risk of tarnishing your shining image. Whenever we made a presentation to a prospective client or heard that they had hired our advertising agency, we immediately were ready to set up an appointment to begin planning strategy and tactics. If you are selling a product, you should know the delivery schedule by heart so you can tell your new customer the exact date they will receive their purchase.

❐ Frequently Asked Questions (FAQ) List

No matter what you sell, you will have to answer questions about your product or service. As you make more sales calls and gain experience you'll find a number of questions reoccurring on a predictable basis. These are the Frequently Asked Questions. In the less stressful atmosphere of your office you can reflect on these and prepare your best answers. If you work with other salespeople, ask them about their FAQs and trade answers. You might uncover some areas in which you are vague or incomplete in your presentations. Your files of FAQs will not only help you be ready for customer questions but can also be a guide to better sales presentations.

Until you have mastered each of these points in depth you should never enter a potential customer's office. Obviously, knowing your product is essential to selling it. But there are additional benefits to having superior product or service knowledge.

The first is confidence. When you really know your material, your confidence soars and projects to everyone you meet. You aren't afraid of confronting a tough question because there are no gaps in your knowledge that can be exposed.

Another advantage of extensive product knowledge is that it builds trust between the buyer and seller. In selling a service where the salesperson will be the service provider or supervisor, just imagine the impression left if you don't show superior knowledge from the outset of your presentation. You most likely won't have a customer. On the other hand, a potential customer begins the relationship with trust in your abilities as you show a firm grasp of your services and what benefits they deliver to clients. This initial trust only intensifies over time as the client sees you in action putting your knowledge to work.

Thirdly, superior product knowledge increases your personal value to your employer and your customer. In today's world of virtual corporations and outsourcing, knowledge is power. Get all you can. The introvert trait of being studious and inquisitive about things pays off in the extra value you present to employers and customers alike. And remember in the present topsy-turvy business world of mergers, acquisitions and downsizing today's client may be tomorrow's employer.

Finally, as a product or service expert, you decrease buyers' phobias about salespeople. Perhaps they aren't as enlightened as you are about the true nature of sales and still have a negative reaction to anyone trying to "sell" them something. If you're perceived as an expert come to help them solve a problem, your reception will be much more positive.

---

*Introvert Alert*

Your superior product knowledge is a great conversation starter when you feel uncomfortable meeting new people. You can initiate a dialogue by asking questions of your listener that show your level of knowledge and position

---

> you in the listeners mind as a possible source of a solution he or she may need. That established, the conversation can proceed in a direction most beneficial to you. You don't need be concerned about how to begin the conversation. Ask a good question and the rest is easy.

The best way to stay on top of product knowledge is to read, read, read. If you work for a large company, there are probably numerous opportunities to take advantage of on-going training programs and continuing education classes. And if you work in a profession, you most likely have requirements for earning continuing education credits yearly. But don't stop there. Not only learn about your industry; learn more about your customer's industry. Don't just read your trade journals on a regular basis, read your customer's trade journals.

And don't forget the competition. Even though it may be very difficult to stay aware of the competition, your efforts will be well rewarded. A sales person who is prepared to offset competitive moves is in a superior selling position. Just remember, never disparage the competition directly. Instead of saying, "Those dummies at Tweedle Dum company didn't have the brains to include a manual override to their new automatic stacking machine, but we did, " wouldn't it be even better to approach the situation like this: "I'm surprised that Tweedle Dum didn't include a manual override to their new automatic stacking machine. They usually do a better job than that. We make sure we don't overlook those type details and we didn't miss this one."

One word of caution. Just because you possess a great deal of product knowledge doesn't mean you should give it all away. Provide enough to show your prospect that you are on top of the subject and that even greater information will be transferred once they sign on the dotted line. Too often, inexperienced introvert salespeople will perform a "brain drain" for their prospects intended to show the depth of their knowledge. As a result, the prospect sees no further benefit to becoming a customer and doesn't buy.

## Summary

As I've shown, having great knowledge about your product or service helps to build your confidence and your prospect's image of you at the same time. Having this superior knowledge can be the introvert's secret advantage over other salespeople. It also can help you take the focus off you and put it where it belongs, on the benefits your product or service offers the buyer. Create your own product knowledge checklist from the above and review it periodically to make sure you don't become complacent about your product or service.

# Chapter 7

# Pillar #4: Building Personal Relationships with Clients

No matter what you are selling, building a personal relationship with your direct buyer is extremely important for your long-term success. The old adage that people buy from people they like has been true in my experience. And one of the keys to having people like you is showing that you are interested in them. The more you know about your buyer, the better you can show your interest and build a relationship.

It begins with knowledge. In his best-selling *Swim with the Sharks Without Being Eaten Alive*, author and lecturer Harvey Mackay offered 66 questions that every salesperson should be able to answer about his customers. But even before I read Mackay's prescription for building relationships, I was acquainted with a printing company in St. Louis that utilized a four-page form to accumulate information on everything from children, education, work objective, hobbies and drink preferences to favorite vacation spots. Every salesperson was required to collect this information on each of their accounts and keep it in a central file accessible to the sales manager. As the salesperson worked with his customer, he had information with which to make small talk, information that indicated his interest in the individual customer. He knew what to say and what not to say. Over time, he could better understand the customer, his business and personal motivations just by obtaining answers to the questions posed by the form. While this information helped the salespeople build relationships, it also was invaluable should they leave the company. It made training a new person easier and gave them a head start in taking over the account. As we have seen, the information provided by the exiting sales person can be a key to a successful transition to a new salesperson on important accounts.

Remember what I said about having information about a prospect or customer before you make an initial sales call? Wouldn't it have been an overwhelmingly positive beginning to a relationship if that new salesperson had called me and said, "I understand you are from St. Louis; you know, that's one of my most favorite cities." Wow. Immediate contact.

With a slight apology to Mackay, I've compiled what I feel to be the 25 most essential pieces of personal information that are useful in getting to know a customer. You won't be able to fill it in completely after your first or probably your second meeting, but over time it should be your objective to have a complete file on each of your customers.

---

### Introvert Alert

While the emphasis here is on finding out information about your prospect and customer, don't be afraid to let them know who you are too. It will help them be more comfortable with you and make small talk even easier. You might find some areas of mutual interest such as kids, pets, hobbies etc. It also makes you look less the grand inquisitor, asking an endless stream of questions, if you provide some information about yourself. As they know you better, they will probably like you better too!

---

A note of caution. There will be people who prefer to keep you at arm's distance. Of course you can't push too hard at this point. As we'll discuss in the chapter on flexibility, you need to be aware of your prospect's comfort zone as well as your own. Watch out for signs that your prospects are uncomfortable talking about certain areas of their lives and move away from them as quickly as possible. Note what areas are out-of-bounds in your file and make sure to avoid them in the future.

On a positive note, I've found most people have areas of their lives that immediately bring out pride and enjoyment whenever they are mentioned. Children, pets, hobbies and volunteer work are usually these type areas. When you find these subjects, be sure to include them in your small talk and correspondence with your customer.

## Murphy's 25 Most Important Pieces of Customer Personal Information

### Personal

1. Customer Name _____

   Role in Company _____

   Nickname _____

   Use it?  ☐ Yes  ☐ No

2. Company Name _____

3. Address _____

   Phone _____

   Fax _____

   e-mail _____

4. Assistant's name and phone _____

   _____

5. Home address _____

   Home Phone _____

6. Birth date and Place _____

7. Physical Characteristics _____

8. Marital Status _____
   Wife's name _____
   Occupation _____

9. Children and ages _____
   _____
   _____

10. Hobbies _____
    Clubs _____

11. Professional Organizations _____

12. Education _____
    Fraternity or Sorority _____
    Collegiate Sports _____

13. Armed Services _____

## Business

14. Previous Positions in Company _____

15. Previous Employment _____
    _____
    _____

16. Personal business objectives _____

17. Currently reports to _____

18. Significant stock ownership _____

## Lifestyle

19. Does customer drink alcohol? _____
    Offended by others drinking alcohol? _____

20. Does customer object to having anyone buy his/her meal?
    _____

21. Favorite place for lunch _____

    Dinner _____

22. Enjoys spectator sports? _____

    Which teams? _____

24. Cars _____

25. Politics _____

Here are two examples of using customer personal information to build relationships:

When I took a job as advertising manager at an auto parts company, I inherited a printing salesman who had produced the large catalogs that were part of that business at the time. During one of our early conversations he found that I loved golf but was a, shall we say, less than scratch golfer (about 20 strokes less than scratch to be exact). In short, I lost a lot of golf balls whenever I played.

This fellow lived across from a golf course and during his morning walks he picked up a lot of errant balls that fell in his yard or in his neighbors' yards. He began to bring the lost golf balls to me on each visit and it became a tradition between us. I appreciated his bringing the balls to me much more than I would have if he had bought packages of golf balls for me. It was a warm, human gesture that helped to build a solid relationship between us.

Did he still have to have the lowest price to get printing contracts? Yes, but I gave him every opportunity to meet the lowest price and he usually did.

The next example was a graphic artist I worked with early in my career. About this time, my wife and I had our first child, a boy. The artist naturally heard about this wonderful child from the proud father each time we talked. One day he brought in a hand-made wooden car that he had made for my son. What a great gift! It didn't cost a lot, so it didn't raise any eyebrows about impropriety. But it was from the heart and my son still has it many years later. That gift deepened my relationship with the artist as we did many other projects together.

The moral of these stories is that, if you try, you can find special ways to acknowledge the specialness of your customers and build relationships that can lead to years of very profitable business for you.

## Entertaining

Most of us introverts don't take well to entertaining clients. The structured relationship of seller and buyer is more easily managed than the forced camaraderie of customer schmoozing. But that doesn't mean we can't be successful at entertaining our clients. We just have to take an introvert-friendly approach that comes from within ourselves. Find something that you are interested in, at least mildly. In other words, don't go to the ballet with a customer if you abhor the ballet. Get him tickets by all means. But don't go yourself. If you do, you'll come across as phony and untrue to yourself. You'll probably have a lousy time and so will your customer. However, if you like the ballet, find out if your customer does and invite him or her. In short, probe for areas of mutual interest and then base your entertaining on those mutual interests.

Don't hesitate to use lunch to combine entertaining and meetings. When I was a buyer, I appreciated going out to lunch with suppliers. It got me out of the office and allowed us a chance to talk. It didn't have to be anything fancy. In fact, I was always suspicious of salespeople that went overboard on lunch. One other point. For me, lunch was something I did with people I knew. I didn't like to go to lunch with people I didn't know. I preferred the office for "get acquainted" meetings. Not everyone is like me, but make sure your prospect likes to lunch on the first date. And if they turn you down, don't take it seriously.

## Summary

As we've seen, building a personal relationship with your customers can have a profound affect on your ultimate success. The best way to build relationships is to show interest in your customers and their lives both in business and away from the job. Having this information will make it much easier to make small talk with your customers and facilitate lunches and other entertaining, if that is appropriate in your business. Begin compiling your information and find your customers points of pride. Use them frequently and your customers will equate you with good, positive feelings. That's not a bad way to begin a sales call.

# Chapter 8

# Pillar #4: Persistence

No other area of selling has spawned as much "how-to" literature as the concept of being aggressive and continuing on in the face of adversity. It seems that every sales book devotes chapter after chapter to the subject of burnout, call reluctance, procrastination or whatever term the author wants to use. Motivational speakers such as Anthony Robbins and Tom Hopkins "preach" the gospel of being aggressive and overcoming call reluctance in giant rallies, in books and on tapes to the tune of millions of dollars yearly.

Much of the need for this motivational canon is due to the fact selling is a very difficult occupation, especially when viewed as a win or lose proposition ¾ the sales person vs. the buyer. Many salespeople still buy that old paradigm of waging war against the buyer. When you are constantly facing an "enemy" your spirit and your body will eventually give out. The result is a dispirited sales person and more book and seminar revenue for Robbins, Hopkins, and the other legions of sales trainers.

The word "aggressive" is the embodiment of this outlook, similar to "overcoming" objections and "closing" a sale, as we will discuss later. To me the word "persistent" reflects the real attitude it takes to be successful in sales without all the warfare baggage of other terms.

Look at the job listings for salespeople in the Sunday newspaper. Of course, many listings still ask for "aggressive" salespeople. But look more closely. The ads for larger companies and professional firms are moving away from using the term "aggressive." They are looking for people who can build relationships and approach selling from a win-win perspective.

This new approach benefits those of us who are more introverted because we are already perceived as being less aggressive than extroverts. I believe introverts are thought to be less aggressive because aggressiveness is often associated with physical movement and action. You can see aggressiveness. It's hard to see persistence. The introvert does more of his or her work internally, thinking, strategizing. As we will see, the introvert salesperson does more up-front work and spends less time chasing unlikely targets. On a percentage basis, the introvert salesperson will see fewer prospects but will turn a higher percentage into customers.

To me, persistence connotes an internal drive, a positive push toward accomplishing a goal. Aggression carries with it the hint of physical violence and pursuit of a target in order to destroy it. This can have negative connotations to the pursued target. When I perceive that some one is being aggressive toward me, I take it negatively. Don't you? Persistence is a better word to describe someone who has my needs in mind and will continue to work toward fulfilling those needs out of a conviction that they have a solution to my need or desire.

An example of what I mean by persistence is my experience with one of my favorite former advertising agency accounts. It just so happened that a previous colleague of mine was named the marketing director for a home heating equipment manufacturer near St. Louis. In visiting with my friend, I found that the company had a relationship with an advertising agency and was happy with the service and marketing materials they were receiving from that company. In fact, the agency account executive had worked with my friend's new company for over ten years.

It didn't take a genius to decide that my short-term prospects for unseating the incumbent were not too good at that point. However, I knew that every situation changes and I was determined to be there when the opportunity presented itself. For almost two years I met with my contact at least quarterly. I let him know I was interested in his business by sending him articles from trade magazines and by keeping him updated on my agency.

Finally, one day at lunch, my friend said he was concerned about the billing from his present agency. That was all I needed. I persuaded him to let my agency work up a cost comparison between his present agency and mine. When he saw the difference, it was a piece of cake. I had a new client and he had lower costs with comparable or even better creativity.

That's what I mean by persistence.

Would a more aggressive, in your face approach have lessened the time it took to acquire the account? I don't think so. When trying to unseat a well-entrenched incumbent, timing is everything. An ill-timed assault from the old paradigm of selling would have been deadly. Aggression would have brought about a battle when my competitor was strong, a battle I would have lost. Instead of creating a battle, I concentrated on listening to my prospect, hoping to recognize a need that was not being met by the other agency. By focusing on my prospect, I was showing that I cared and was ready to help when he needed it.

However, I don't mean to say that you should simply wait on the sidelines until your target prospect calls you. I have another example of persistence, but this one didn't have a happy ending for my firm. A major industrial company in Portland sent out Requests for Proposals (RFPs) to all the major accounting firms, mine included. When the RFP hit our door everyone was excited at the prospect of signing a major new audit client. As you might imagine, a great amount of work went into preparing the proposal, meeting with the prospect and developing an oral presentation. But after all was said and done, my firm was not selected. Instead, the company hired a firm that had been courting them for over three years, doing all the "little things" that had kept them on the prospects radar screens, like calling at regular intervals, providing timely information on relevant subjects and generally keeping in touch. The RFP to the other accounting firms was no more than a formality. We couldn't overcome a relationship that was built over three years.

One of my mentors in the advertising business told me that it was imperative to always have a major account or two waiting in the wings, one that would not surprise you by calling and saying they were ready to make a change. The challenge is to always be working on this "on-deck" account even when your present clients are keeping you busy. We all must never forget that, no matter how good we are, we will lose business through mergers, changes in personnel and other events that are beyond our control. The bright side is that your competitors will lose business too. Make sure you are in a position to pick up the pieces when your competitors falter and lose business.

## Keys to Persistence

While you are waiting for your long-term projects to call you with their business, you'll need to make sure your attitude doesn't falter. Part of being persistent is keeping in the ball game and not giving up in the early innings. Here are four keys to remaining persistent in pursuing your prospects.

**An Attitude of Success.** You have to feel that you are going to be successful. Very few of us can keep working toward a goal unless we really believe we have a chance of attaining it. I'm always amazed that people who overcome great odds to achieve a goal invariably attribute their success to having the attitude that they would win, even when the odds were terribly against them. Remember that having a winning attitude is not an extrovert or introvert domain. Everyone has to believe in themselves and their ability, if they intend to win.

Some of us have this optimism built-in at birth. Some of us don't. I have to tell you that I did not. Quite the contrary. However, you are not alone in this battle. There are excellent outside sources to keep your attitude positive. Writers from Dale Carnegie to Tony Robbins have helped me from one time to another. Find someone or something that works to keep you positive, be it faith, motivational speakers and writers, family and friends — whatever works for you.

**Clear-cut goals.** You have to know what you want to attain or else you'll never know if you've been successful. Most sales training books talk at length about goal setting, so I won't, except to say that goals are of utmost importance in almost every endeavor in life. Some of the same sources as shown above for attitude readjustment can also help you to set goals that will keep you motivated and moving forward in the face of sometimes great odds.

**Reality Check.** This may seem like backtracking after the first two keys to persistence, but it really isn't. My goal of having my friend's advertising account was attainable, given time and human nature. But if I had a goal of pitching for the Cardinals when I was almost 40 years old and hadn't pitched since I was a teenager, that would not be attainable. A reality check on my part would have told me as much. Don't set your sites too low, but do keep reality in mind.

**Plan.** A goal is only a dream without a plan to achieve it. Figure out how best to achieve the results you want and then follow your instincts. Know what you are going to do along the way to achieve your goal. Be ready to push ahead as you pass each signpost along the way. Going back to my friend's advertising account, I knew in my heart that my agency was a better value for him, so I devised a plan that I followed over time. I knew that the best way to show him our value was to have him compare costs on an actual job. I looked for just such an opening by talking with him regularly and asking the type questions that would uncover any dissatisfaction he was having with his previous agency's billing. When my opening came I was ready.

---

### Introvert Alert

Don't take "no" personally and be aware of negativity creeping into your self-talk. No matter how good we are at selling, we still receive our share of No's. After a number of rejections, it's human nature to begin to doubt our abilities. Be prepared by taking advantage of inspirational tapes, books and seminars. There is nothing wrong with using them for coaching and keeping your attitude positive. Many people are born with the attitude that a room full of horse manure means there is a pony nearby. Congratulations to them! For the rest of us, it takes continual reinforcement to keep our hopes up and moving in the right direction. Make your library of coaches an integral part of your business day.

---

## Voice Mail Hell

One of the toughest tests of our persistence is getting through to someone in this day of pervasive voice mail. It seems that no one answers his or her phone anymore. Instead we are greeted with the promise that the owner of the recorded voice will get back to us as soon as possible. Sure.

But facing voice mail doesn't have to be a totally negative experience. In fact, it can offer an opportunity to convey our sales message when we might have otherwise been unable to do so. Compare the following phone messages:

Hi. This is Jim Jones with JJ Public Relations. Could you give me a call at 444-4444.
Hi. This is Jim Jones with JJ Public Relations. I would

like to talk with you regarding a crisis management program. My number is 444-4444.

Hi. This is Jim Jones with JJ Public Relations. My firm specializes in helping companies like yours to prepare for any number of crises that could cripple your business. I can show you how to avoid a catastrophe. I'm at 444-4444. I look forward to talking over your situation. That's Jim Jones at 444-4444. Thank you.

I think we would all agree that the last one is vastly superior. But, really, how many times do you hear messages like that. In my experience too many are like the first one, offering little or no incentive to return the call.

How many of you are totally prepared to face voice mail when you make a phone sales call? I expect that most of us just reach for the phone and dial, then improvise a quick message when we hear the familiar, "Leave a message..." That's wasting a great opportunity. Instead of just "winging it, " why not prepare a concise statement of the nature of the call with an emphasis on the benefit to the receiver? Most of us have simply too many phone messages to try to decipher some incomplete and insufficient request for a return call.

Tell the listener the benefit he or she will accrue by returning your call. Think of your listener as having five messages spread before her. Each requests a return call and she has only time to make one call. Which one will she make? The message that offers the greatest benefit will be the one that's returned.

Another idea is to follow up an important phone message with a fax that includes a couple of your biggest benefits and reinforces the need for the recipient to contact you. Just be careful you don't offend anyone. In many instances, unsolicited fax mail can be perceived negatively.

## Summary

I can't emphasize the need for persistence enough. As introverts we don't crave the approval of others on a daily basis. It is all too easy to withdraw back into ourselves if our efforts are not initially successful. But the truth is that selling does require the action and approval of others if a sale is to be made. We cannot and should not take rejection personally but learn to separate our intrinsic worth from our sales efforts. Whether an introvert or an extrovert, a salesperson must be willing to be persistent in working toward a sale if they are to be successful. You don't have to be overtly aggressive, but you do have to be persistent.

# Chapter 9

# Flexibility

One of the most valuable assets for any sales person to possess is the ability to "read" people. In theory, introverts should actually be better at this than extroverts because by being quiet and less obtrusive, they have the opportunity to listen more and get a better read on the person they are speaking with. Armed with this information they can then adjust their own demeanor accordingly.

Remember, we said people tend to like people they believe are like themselves. Opposites don't attract. In fact, they repel. You want to be as much like your prospect as possible within the boundaries of your own comfort level. Step out of those boundaries and you run the risk of appearing foolish or, even worse, you might be perceived as mocking your listener.

In the final analysis, all really good salespeople, introvert or extrovert, are flexible to some extent. They have the ability to read clients and prospects and to subtly adjust their appearance, presentation and emphasis to mirror their prospective buyer. Sure, it's probably easier for an extrovert to sell to an extrovert and an introvert to sell to an introvert. But true success demands the ability to sell to anyone; no matter what type personality they may possess.

I'm not saying you have to be a chameleon looking to your

customer for your own personality. It is much subtler than that. On the physical level it may mean moving just a bit more quickly, speaking with a faster cadence, and sitting a bit closer to someone than you usually do. This challenge isn't confined to introverts exclusively. The intelligent extrovert, upon ascertaining that his prospect doesn't share his devotion to a frenetic pace, moves a bit more slowly, tones down his speech and sits just a bit further back from the desk. The key is to be aware of your prospect's or customer's style and adjust accordingly.

Sometimes this can be painful, literally. My most difficult situation concerned the president of a division of a Fortune 1000 company that my agency represented. He was a bear of a man, quite taken with himself. He had been very successful in business from an early age. He was quick-minded and witty. In dealing with him I always cranked up my energy level a bit and tried to be more demonstrative in my movements. But he had one trait I couldn't emulate.

In short he was a "belly-bumper." Believe it or not, if one of us made a particularly insightful remark, or he liked a piece of artwork presented to him, he would rise from his chair and expect you to exchange "belly-bumps" with him. Besides being embarrassing, it was difficult for me due to his large size and forcefulness. It was all anyone could do to stay upright after being bumped by him. I never felt comfortable doing this and tried to avoid it at all costs. I finally solved the problem by bringing a designated "belly-bumper" with me whenever I met with this individual. Usually the designee was a junior member of the art staff that I would drag unsuspectingly to the meetings. I would sit grinning while my pinch-hitter was "belly-bumped." The moral of this "belly-bumping" tale is that there is always a way to be flexible in dealing with even the most bizarre of clients.

## Reading People

There is no shortage of books on how to read people. Self-help books can show you how to take your cues from indicators such as office layout and decorations, body language and business dress. I suggest you invest the time to learn more about the intricacies of reading people and personality styles. As introverts, we should enjoy the challenge and opportunity to learn something new about people and put it into use.

For our purposes, and in the short run, I would advise you to focus on three signs of a person's character: their office, their speech patterns and their physical position when talking to you.

## The Office

The office is easy. The sparser the office, the more likely the person wants to get down to business quickly without a lot of small talk and introduction. Just give these types the facts. Don't start out telling the story of your company founding in 1932. Get to the point quickly and explain your best benefits first. With someone like this, it is a good idea to tell the person how long you expect to need and then stick to it. Rambling and long drawn out presentations are your enemies here.

If your prospect's office is full of material but sorted into piles and neatly stacked, you've got a detail person. You probably still need to be highly focused but be sure to take the time to include all the details of your product or service. As long as you stick to the subject and provide substance, you'll have an audience. But be prepared for questions. Detail people like details, details, details. Make your answers comprehensive and always ask if they need further refinement.

If your prospect has a generally messy office with papers strewn here and there, the photos a little crooked on the wall and a couple of old coffee cups on the window sill, you've probably got someone more creative, more easy going, a big picture person. So most likely you can take a few moments to warm up, tell a few stories and take your time asking questions or explaining details. Don't rush with these people. You'll take more time but should be richly rewarded.

## Speech Patterns

Speech is also a telling sign of our internal makeup. In general, just be aware of your prospect's speech patterns and try to move your own natural patterns closer to theirs. If he or she is a fast talker, speed up your patterns of speech. Conversely, if they speak slowly and methodically, you do the same, as much as feels comfortable to you. Never stray too far from your comfort zone because you will feel unnatural and it will project to your listener.

## Position

Body language is much more difficult than speech to interpret. Of course, crossed arms and legs are signs of resistance and arms and legs relaxed are signs of acceptance. But it has been my experience that body language can be so changeable and affected by so many variables that it is better to control your own body language than to constantly try to adjust yourself to your prospect. So always be sure that you are open, looking directly at your prospects and leaning slightly toward them. But be sure to always leave a respectable space between you and the person with whom you are speaking. Nothing can be more disconcerting to a person that likes their space than someone who sits too close for comfort.

Over the years, I have worked with a few salespeople who have had an annoying habit of getting too close to me when talking. In my experience, these were usually extroverts, "touchy, feely" types. But getting too close is not only an extrovert problem. After all, we introverts appreciate our own personal space and are not as prone to invading others' personal territory. But what I have found is that introverts who are not comfortable in a selling situation can react to their nervousness by getting "up close and personal" and be just as obnoxious as any extrovert that gets too close.

Be watchful of how your listener reacts. Start out where you feel comfortable and then adjust as you take your cues from the other person. If they appear to like you closer, then by all means move closer. But if they are like me and don't want you too close, stay back and make sure they are comfortable.

---

*Introvert Alert*

Because we introverts navigate by our own compasses, we can be susceptible to stubbornness. You need to be sure you are aware of others and be flexible in dealing with them. If your prospect has just had a double latte and keeps looking at his watch, don't continue to talk slowly and go through your entire sales pitch. Give 'em the basics, ask your questions and get out. However, be sure to have a reason to come back. You should be stubborn about one thing though...keep smiling.

---

## Flexibility Checklist

Assess your prospects and customers on each of these issues and make sure you understand and reflect their preferences in the following areas:

Customer Name _____

Dress _____

*(eg., Suit, sport coat and slacks, shirtsleeves, dresses, pantsuits, boots)*

Voice _____

*(eg., soft spoken, loud, quick talker, paced)*

Body Language _____

*(eg., up close and personal, keep your distance, informal, formal, uses hands, doesn't use hands)*

Energy Level _____

*(eg., high, low, varies with time of day, affected by stress)*

Humor_____

*(eg., Likes to tell jokes, likes to hear jokes, avoid humor, dry wit)*

Entertainment _____

    *(eg., lunch, breakfast, sporting events, theater, with spouses/ without spouses)*

Subjects to avoid _____

    *(Eg.politics, marriage, health)*

## Voice Check

Your voice is a remarkable communications tool, conveying not only words, but also emotions. When your tone matches your words it can be a powerful combination for delivering a precise and persuasive message to your listeners. But when your words and tone of voice don't match, you leave your listeners confused at best and quite possibly with the wrong impression.

Here are a few common problem areas in speaking. Make sure you aren't guilty of committing these avoidable sins.

**Apathetic.** You just don't seem to care about your listener and recite a sales message by rote.

Rushed. All you want is to get through your presentation and get to the "close." How does that make your listener feel?

**Phony.** Is there anything more upsetting than phony sweetness either in person or on the phone?

**Hesitant.** Nothing helps to erode trust more than being hesitant and halting in your speech. The listener is left wondering if you know what you are talking about or if you are unsure about the information you are attempting to convey.

Be sure your voice carries energy and enthusiasm at all times; in person, on the phone and in your voice messages. You'll leave a lasting positive impression with everyone you come into contact with.

Also be sure to check your voice for the following:

**Articulation.** Can people understand you? We all have some words that might be more difficult for us to say and for others to understand. Ask your co-workers or family to alert you to any problem words or phrases.

**Pitch.** No one likes a monotone voice without pitch or inflection. Tape yourself and listen for fluctuations in pitch. If you don't hear any, your clients won't either. You need to work on making your voice sound interesting.

**Volume.** Extremes of loudness or softness are irritating and distracting to communication. If you see people moving away or edging closer when you talk to them, that's a good indication you need to make some changes.

Don't take your voice for granted. It might just be a missing link in your personal success formula.

## Summary

As we've discussed, being flexible is an essential asset for any salesperson. Speech patterns, dress, physical proximity and your voice can all affect how others perceive you and how they react to your sales messages. By being aware of others and making subtle adjustments in your own style, you'll find your prospects and customers "warming" to you as you "warm" to them.

Part 3

# Opportunities for Introvert Salespeople

# Chapter 10

# Sales Skills for a New Millennium

The world of selling has changed considerably over the last ten years. Old selling wisdom, typified by the "Win ning through intimidation" approach, has been discredited and new paradigms of success, as seen by book titles such as *Relationship Selling*, and *Partnership Selling*, have been recognized. Even if popular culture still portrays every sales person as the stereotypical "shove it down their throat" used car salesman; the real world of selling is vastly different and now places great value on individuals who possess personalities and character traits we usually identify with introverts.

Let's take a look at five major changes in the selling environment that have had a significant impact on the way salespeople actually sell, thereby creating a greater need for introverts in the selling process.

### Buyer Wariness

Or should I say weariness. Advertising and selling messages literally bombard us daily. TV, magazines, telemarketing, radio, billboards and direct mail. It seems that every day there are even more selling intrusions into our lives. Shopping carts have ads, movies have ads, sporting events are an orgy of advertising, and marketers attempting to build brands among teenagers and other school-age children are even invading schools. There's an ever-increasing amount of advertising on the Internet and sales messages greet you when you are waiting on hold on the telephone. According to Business Week, the average American was exposed to over 3,000 sales messages a day in 1991. That number has most likely increased substantially since then.

Why, even rest rooms aren't safe. Water Closet Media in Portland exclusively sells eye level restroom advertising that "demands the undivided attention of a captive audience." Their promotional material quotes a Rice University study that says, "consumers spend significant time reading rest room ads with no distractions." Is there no escape?

In New York recently, a company proposed beaming advertising logos and slogans onto sidewalks to be viewed by pedestrians. It seems no square inch of the consumers' field of view is to be left without a sales message.

In reaction to this, Americans are increasingly looking for ways to protect themselves from unwanted selling messages. Caller ID on telephones, and VCRs with built-in ad zappers are part of this desire. It took Bell Atlantic eight years to sell its first one million caller ID units, but only one year to sell the second one million. The major car companies now offer on-line buying opportunities, partly for timesaving but also to bypass the salesperson. Many cities and states have passed ordinances against unwanted telephone soliciting and door-to-door selling. A recent NBC news segment on home repair rip-offs advised buyers never to do business with a company that contacts you by phone. The consumer's overriding sentiment is one of skepticism and annoyance toward unwanted sales intrusions.

This attitude follows the consumer to work where the business-to-business buyer has the same wariness and weariness toward high-pressure selling in the office. The glut of direct mail, phone calls, voice mails, e-mails and other solicitations is a rude intrusion into an increasingly busy workday.

As a result of this buyer wariness, the sale professional who can project a non-sales, non-threatening image is at an advantage. The new sales paradigm is that of a consultant or of a doctor, someone to listen to the consumer's needs and offer solutions. To do this, the sales person/consultant must be highly intelligent and have great listening skills. The fast-talking, "slap 'em on the back" sales pro is the last thing the consumer wants. At the first wink of the eye, consumers erect their defenses and slip back behind their protective walls.

A local Saturn dealer plays into this consumer mind-set with an ad that shows a tire pressure gauge and promises "Way more pressure than you'll get from our consultants." The copy promises that "we let every customer make their own decision whether to buy or not. Because unlike tires, people don't come with instructions indicating how much hot air they can take."

If auto dealers are getting message, the rest of us should take note.

### Better Educated and Informed Buyers

The second major change in the sales culture is that the American public is better educated than at any time in the past, thus increasing the sophistication and knowledge shown by buyers both in consumer selling and in business to business transactions. The numbers for Oregon are typical of the country as a whole. In 1980, 18% of Oregonians over 25 years old had completed baccalaureate degrees. In 1996, that number had increased to 29%. In 1980, 76% of the state's residents over the age of 25 had completed high school or an equivalent program. In 1996, that number had increased to 91%.

As American become better educated there are additional opportunities to gain even more knowledge. The Internet and World Wide Web are the most obvious, but cable and satellite television, the publication of more specialized magazines and the affordability of CD-roms have all had an impact on the amount of raw information available to everyone. The Information Highway is a reality.

Today, it's not unusual for a car buyer to walk into a showroom with a printout of dealer costs from the Internet and a copy of Consumer Reports. According to Business Marketing Magazine, a full 20% of new car shoppers now visit car company web sites prior to visiting a show room. It is predicted that the number will reach 50% in a few years. You aren't going to pressure these informed consumers into a premature decision. Gone are the days when buying a car was about as enjoyable as root canal work. The advent of no-dicker pricing, hiring of salaried salespeople, a growing emphasis on customer satisfaction and the whole Saturn marketing program reflect this new selling environment. Similar changes are taking place in other consumer industries.

In business-to-business selling, the single purchasing agent is being replaced by buying teams that may include engineering, finance and even marketing. The days of the lowest product price and a bottle of scotch for the purchasing manager at Christmas are long gone.

The increasing use of outside consultants also has increased buyers' knowledge level. In industry after industry, consultants with particular expertise are being employed to manage projects that include purchasing products or services. As you might expect, these consultants will only work with salespeople who can exhibit a high level of knowledge and help them do their job for their client. The result is the need for smarter and smarter salespeople — detail-oriented, knowledgeable salespeople.

I once had a package conveyor company as a client. The salespeople, or sales engineers as they were called, were some of the most intelligent, knowledgeable people I have ever met. As a group they weren't shrinking violets, but they certainly didn't fit the stereotype of the extrovert sales person either. It isn't news that there are sales positions like this. What is new is that these type sales positions are expanding rapidly as business becomes more sophisticated. The sales person who can communicate specialized knowledge in a clear, concise, customer benefit focused manner will be the sales star of the future.

I have had a number of clients in the electric motor business. When I first started working with motor companies, it was a catalog and price book business. The sales person needed to know some facts about motors and electricity, but the majority of the information that was needed to make a sale was found in the catalog and price book Today, customization is the most important aspect of motor manufacturing. With the adoption of advanced techniques for assembly and distribution, almost every customer can have a special motor that they, in essence, design. The salesperson is usually part of that design team. He or she has to have an intimate knowledge of electricity, motors, the company's capabilities and the customers needs. The price book and catalog have been exchanged for a laptop, modem and knowledgeable sales person.

## Long-term Partnerships

The third change in the selling environment is the emphasis on long-term partnerships. Businesses are increasingly recognizing the value of retaining customers over time. In many cases, retaining a present customer presents 3 or 4 times the financial return compared to the cost of attracting a new customer. In the consumer area, we see frequent flyer, diner, buyer and copier programs, all designed to reward present customers for staying on board. Small business also sees the advantages of retaining clients. My barber offers a free haircut with every ten purchased. My favorite coffee stop offers a similar frequent use promotion. Even these small businesses recognize the importance of repeat customes.

In business-to-business marketing we see companies using fewer suppliers but developing much closer relationships to them. Technology like Electronic Data Interchange (EDI) makes it possible for suppliers to directly access retail sales activity and automatically ship merchandise as needed to their customers' locations. These types of relationships are built on trust, knowledge and mutual understanding. Once a company selects a supplier, invests the time and money to train them and shares the technology needed for inter-company communications, they don't change suppliers very often.

Of course, the skills needed to service and retain existing customers are not necessarily the same as those needed to attract new customers. In the advertising business, as in most businesses, there was a group of "rain makers." They knew everybody and could get an appointment with anyone. I'm sure they were all extroverts. They were constantly called upon whenever there was an urgent need for new clients. However, the new clients they brought in were a reflection of themselves: short sighted, looking for the short-term advantage. For the most part, the rainmakers and their itinerant clients were gone as quickly as they came. The substantial, long-term client came on board as a result of continuing efforts by dedicated, knowledgeable people within the organization, maybe even an introvert or two.

## The End of Product Solutions

The fourth influence on sales culture is the decreasing emphasis on basic products and services. A word we hear constantly today is solution - as in "we provide solutions. A "solution" in this context has three components: first is the basic product or service; second is the on-going customer service that accompanies the basic product; and third is "added value." This can best be explained by two examples.

I worked in the accounting business where the audit is the basic product. Information on how to address accounting questions and problems throughout the year is the on-going service. The added value is the experience in a particular industry that the lead client service partner offers the client. It might also be focused expertise in an accounting subject such as the procedures for a company to sell stock to the public.

In the real estate business, the listing and showing of your home to prospective buyers is the product. The sharing of timely information on the number of people viewing your home and the preparation of the paperwork involved with formal purchase offers are the on-going service. The agent's ability to get below market financing or to find a reputable carpenter for those last minute home repairs is the added value.

If products and services are all similar, the competition is at the added value level. And, as you can see from these examples, often the added value comes from the experience, focus and detail orientation of the salesperson. In such cases, substance is the introvert's most valuable asset. Successful salespeople are not "hit and run artists" anymore. They are an integral and important part of the overall value a company offers to the buyers of its products or services.

## Busy Consumers

The fifth change affecting selling is how incredibly busy everyone seems to be these days. All the wonders of technology that we've adopted have not led to increased leisure but ironically have made us busier than ever as we try to accomplish more and more in our lives and fulfill our ever rising expectations. As a recent Buick commercial proclaims: "When life is fast, life is good."

At first glance, it might seem those busy consumers and faster business transactions would require the extrovert's strengths in cold calling and aggressive selling. But that is not necessarily true.

In today's environment, people have an incredible amount of tasks to accomplish in both their business and personal lives. To do that, they need to trust and rely upon others to provide solutions to their many needs. They don't have time to change financial advisors yearly. They don't want to spend time finding a new lawyer or accountant. As a result, just as we saw previously, busy people prefer to build long-term relationships with the people they rely on to help them conduct their lives. But the providers of these products or services continually must be on the leading edge of their respective industries, providing the latest in innovations to their customers. Fall behind in your understanding and knowledge of your industry and your buyer will spend the time to get the latest and best, if that is what it takes.

An example of this might be the financial planner who learns about the new Roth IRA and wants to keep his clients informed. A good financial planner will send information to all his clients and maybe even call each one to further explain the main points of the new savings vehicle. But the successful financial planner who really understands his or her clients' busy schedules will take the time to write a proposal based on his or her knowledge of the client's finances. The proposal will show the impact of the new IRA in specific, easy-to-read fashion for the client. All the client has to do is review the figures and make a decision. Much of the work has already been done, thus saving the investor precious time that could be used to make even more money to invest.

Again, the introvert who is super-knowledgeable in his or her industry, dedicated to customer service and persistently engaged with their accounts will be successful. But if you wait for your customer to request the latest and greatest, you could be in trouble. They don't have time to contact you. It's up to you to keep them abreast of your market and running at warp speed.

These five changes combine to make the introvert salesperson much more valuable than at any time in history. It stacks up like this:

| Sales Environment Change | Introvert Advantage |
|---|---|
| Buyer Wariness | Non-threatening approach<br>Likeability |
| Buyer Sophistication | Product Knowledge<br>Tempered reactions |
| Long-term partnerships | Better at one-on-one<br>    relationships<br>Knowledge |

| Sales Environment Change | Introvert Advantage |
|---|---|
| Less emphasis on product solutions | Ability to add value |
| Speed of business | Knowledge<br>On-going relationships |

## Summary

The selling environment reflects many of the changes taking place in business both in the U.S. and throughout the world. Some of these changes have helped to place a higher value on introvert traits such as exceptional product knowledge, the ability to create long-term relationships, and attention to detail. While not every selling position is affected today, the trend is that these five major changes will affect an ever-growing segment of the business world and create even more opportunities for introvert sales success in the new millennium.

In our next chapter, we'll see how the introvert sales person can take advantage of these trends to find new customers and retain existing ones.

# Chapter 11

# Sales Hunting
# Vs. Sales Farming

Over the years that I've been associated with selling, I've identified two major types of salespeople. I divide them into the Hunters and the Farmers. The Hunters tend to be more extroverted. They march forth into the wilderness, armed with 15 killer openings, 32 can't-miss closes, 45 ways to overcome objections, and a heartfelt opinion that they can sell anybody anything. If it moves, they fire at it, sending forth their salvo of aggressive sales bullets. Their biggest problem is finding enough targets to keep them busy shooting. They live for the hunt.

Telemarketers are hunters. Investment tele-salespeople and rookie insurance agents are prolific hunters. And the greatest sales hunters of them all are door-to-door salespeople. Yes, they still exist, even in business-to-business sales. For instance, The National Association of the Self Employed instructs their salespeople to canvass door-to-door in business parks to market their line of benefits and health care for small business owners.

Sales Farmers on the other hand "grow" sales by carefully selecting fertile soil (targeting), planting seeds (various awareness building and lead generating activities) and then harvesting sales (face-to-face selling).

The problem with sales hunting is that it is strictly a numbers game. Typical sales training books say "just make enough cold calls and you'll be successful. Count every 'no' as a step on a ladder of success." No doubt there are individuals who have prospered as sales hunters. They have the personalities and resiliency to keep on in the face of overwhelming odds. Good for them.

Due to the changes in the business environment outlined in the previous chapter, I believe sales hunters are becoming less successful and sales farmers more successful. Sales hunting relies much more on being overtly aggressive and having many of the characteristics of the old stereotypical sales person. Sales hunting discounts building relationships, showing in-depth expertise and listening skills. For the most part, it is the old fast-talking, "have I got a deal for you" sales paradigm.

The good news is that the paradigm for sales success no longer requires "hunting" skills exclusively. For many of us, attempting to be a sales hunter is simply counterproductive. All the time used to get up the courage to make the cold calls, perfect the canned pitch that sounds spontaneous and attempt to see people that are totally disinterested in what we have to sell is a waste. Plus it, in the words of former St. Louis Cardinal's baseball manager Whitey Herzog, "gets our dauber down." Why beat our heads against the wall when there are other, and better, ways to be successful? We introverts are much better sales farmers than sales hunters.

Here are the differences between the sales hunter and sales farmer:

**Sales Farmer**
- Targeting
- Lots of Preparation
- Quality
- Continuous
- Variety of tactics

**Sales Hunter**
- Prospecting
- Lesspreparation
- Quantity
- Episodic
- One tactic

## The Sales Farmer

A sales farmer finds fertile soil upon which to plant the seeds that will produce sales in the future. As the farmer needs to have fertile soil in which to plant the seeds that will produce his crops, the successful introvert salesperson must find the prospects that present the greatest probability of buying. While all successful salespeople need to target, for the introvert it is even more important because his up-front marketing efforts will be more involved and time consuming. He can't afford to waste time on unlikely targets.

The seeds are lead-generating activities such as referrals, advertising, public relations, industry associations and other groups, speaking and writing. All these activities are designed to generate interest in you and bring customers to your doorstep, customers who know you and are interested in your product or service.

Finally, harvesting is making the sale to buyers who are knowledgeable about you and your company and are much more likely to buy from you compared to the targets the hunter tries to bag. Quality vs quantity. Here introverts can put their best traits forward such as knowing their product and customers intimately, building personal relationships one-on-one, taking care of details and having their opinions and views valued.

You may be thinking at this point that planting crops is not very satisfying if you are hungry today. The ravenous sales manager wants more sales today, not in some indefinite future. The sales farming techniques we'll be reviewing produce results at different speeds from immediately to months and years in the future. For instance, a simple letter preceding your phone call can help introduce you and your company to your target thereby warming, however slightly, a cold call.

Here's another way to look at sales farming. The selling process at its simplest consists of four components: awareness, interest, desire, and action. When someone calls you to sell you a new mutual fund, they must first make you aware of the fund, generate some interest in the fund on your part, make its benefits so compelling that you will desire to have the fund and then motivate you to take action by actually buying.

Sales farmers, on the other hand, employ marketing communications techniques such as advertising, public relations, referrals and others, to create awareness and build interest in their products. The actual face-to-face selling only has to accomplish the last two tasks, building desire and asking for action. As a result, the sales farmer's selling time is much more productive compared to the sales hunter who has four tasks to complete before being successful.

Here's an example of how sales farming has worked for me in building my sales and marketing consulting practice. I decided that public speaking would be my main method of planting sales seeds. I have given presentation to many groups over the last year with the intention of accomplishing the first two of the four sales components above, awareness and interest. By the fact I appear before each group as an expert in sales and marketing, I have gained awareness among my audience. Through the content of my talks I build interest in my abilities and solutions to common problems.

When someone comes up to me after my talks and inquires as to my interest and availability to work with their companies, I am usually successful in selling my services to them due to the fact I am already half way to success when we first meet. Compare this to the alternative of calling all these people and saying, in essence, "you don't know me but I have a great idea to make you more successful in your marketing efforts." In my mind, my farming efforts are much more productive than spending my time hunting.

## Targeting

Targeting answers the question, "Who has needs that my product or service can fulfill at a price that is profitable to me?" You must be as specific as possible with your answers because these are the companies and individuals that will be the focus of your lead generating activities.

Every business and sales person needs to have a clear picture of their target before proceeding. However, the sad fact is that many companies don't really do a good job of targeting. They may have a general idea of the companies or individuals to which they sell, but they usually aren't specific enough. Here are some ideas on how to structure a professional targeting program:

**1. Begin with your present customers.**

Retaining your present customers and selling them more of your products or services is 5 times more efficient compared to obtaining new customers. Begin by insuring that you are providing great service to your customers and that they are, in the words of Ken Blanchard "Raving Fans" and enthusiastic supporters of you and your company. Look for additional products or services you can sell to them. It shouldn't be difficult because they know you and the value you deliver to them. Make sure you have a customer retention program in place before you even think of looking for new customers. It will pay great dividends.

Write down the names of at least five customers that you now work with and you are absolutely dedicated to retaining and selling even more to in the future.

_____

_____

_____

_____

_____

**2. Model your "perfect" customer.**

World-class consumer companies employ legions of people to do this, but you can accomplish the same thing in your territory or service area. Simply write down the characteristics of a customer that you would like to have. For my consulting practice, I might describe a "perfect" customer like this:

> Professional services firm, regional to national in scope, 20 plus employees, marketing-oriented, $50,000 minimum marketing/training budget, management committed to growth

That's how I would describe my "perfect" customer. You'll have to give some thought to the attributes that would make up a "perfect" customer for you.

Why don't you do it right now? Take a few moments to reflect on the type company or person that would be a "perfect" prospect for you and your company. Write down the attributes of that company or individual in the space below.

_____

_____

_____

_____

### 3. Find "suspects" that fit the description.

There are any number of sources for this information depending on the targets you want to reach. Directories, phone books, association membership lists and the like can provide the needed candidates. It's important at this point to limit your "suspects" to manageable numbers. If you have too many, you won't do a thorough job with the companies that hold the most potential. You need to find other criteria to sort by until you have a number that is realistic for you. Of course, this is dependent on what you are selling. In the accounting business, we had an A list of ten companies that we felt were good targets for us, plus a B list of another ten companies that didn't have as high a potential. Your manageable list might be 100 companies or one company.

Write down below the names of your top five "suspects" at this point. If the number is less than five, just write down the names of the companies you feel would be great prospects for you.

_____

_____

_____

_____

_____

## 4. Research their needs and fill them

This is the reason you want to keep your numbers small. You want to do as much research as possible on these companies to gain as much useful information as possible to help sell your product or service. You will have a file of information on all these targets and be adding to it at all times. In the course of selling to these companies you will have direct contact with buying influences inside that company. Be sure to keep adding to your file as you gain more direct information.

## 5. Get them into your personal marketing system.

By this I mean that you should have a plan for developing and nurturing contacts within your targets. You should know the name of the buying influences and the names of present suppliers of services similar to your own, i.e. for accounting we always wanted to know the names of bankers, lawyers, investment companies and others who worked with our targets. Be sure to have timely mailings going to influences insider your targets. Even if you work for a large firm and a marketing department does this, be sure your targets are on the appropriate lists and receiving everything the home office is distributing. Start completing your Murphy's 25 for each of the people who will influence your sale. Remember knowledge is power.

## Lead Generation Activities

I use the term lead generation to cover a wide variety of marketing communications actions that you can employ to create awareness of you and your company, and to build interest to the point that prospective customers will contact you for further information about your product or service. At the very least these communications tactics will turn a "cold" call into a "warm" call because the prospect will have heard of you or your company when you contact them. Some of these tactics are designed to produce results quickly and others to attract prospects over a longer period of time. You have to decide which ones are appropriate for you. Usually a mixture of short term and long term projects will keep you busy with new clients and provide a steady stream of prospects for future business.

### Long Term

1. Join and become active in industry groups
2. Use personal public relations
3. Conduct seminars for your target audiences
4. Become recognized as an expert in your field
5. Court Influencers
6. Distribute Newsletters
7. Use the Internet

### 1. Join and Become Active in Industry Groups

The best salespeople are usually active in industry or social organizations that provide opportunities to meet and be seen by potential customers. Some groups such as the Chambers of Commerce or Booster Clubs are mainly networking opportunities. Others are subtler about their networking usefulness. It is usually a good idea to avoid groups of your peers when trolling for customers. Rather, target groups that serve the industries that use your service. An attorney working in the high tech area would join the American Electronics Association, an advertising account executive would join the American Marketing Association. As you become active in the association or group, you'll be able to interact with many people that are potential customers and at the same time learn more about your prospects' industries.

---

### Introvert Alert

When you join an organization, it's a good idea to volunteer for leadership positions. Meetings are good opportunities to network with organization members, but you are usually confined to a short period of time for interaction. As you might expect, introverts probably won't set any records for meeting a large number of people at any one networking event. But by giving extra time to the organization, you will build relationships with other members and also have your name in front of members in meeting announcements and newsletters.

---

### 2. Use Personal Public Relations

You don't have to be a professional PR "flack" to make effective use of public relations. It's simple. Find the media that reaches your target audience and start sending information to them. Here's an example: When we had a flood in Portland, our accounting office developed a booklet on how disasters such as floods affect tax returns. We included IRS publications and even a couple of applicable tax forms. We sent a news release to the media with our tax sales director's name prominently sprinkled throughout the release. The newspaper printed an article on the booklet and quoted extensively from it. It even included our phone number as a contact for getting the books. We had some inquiries from individuals, but we also had a large number from small companies that hired us to help file their tax returns. As an added bonus, a TV station featured one of our tax consultants on a public service program.

Local newspapers are hungry to fill the space between the ads. All they require is that the news is localized. For instance, if you sell commercial air conditioning, you send out a release saying, "Joe Jones, local air conditioning expert, announces new type air conditioning unit available."

Some of you might say, "But I'm not a writer." Don't worry. As an added bonus for reading this book, here's your first and only public relations writing lesson: *Who, What, Where, When, Why* and *How*. Just make sure you answer all of these and you've written a good news release.

And while we are talking about writing, how about writing an article on your product or service for the local newspaper? They love stories about businesses in their distribution areas. They are always looking for important information on new products, new companies and other local news for their papers. And remember, with public relations it doesn't matter that your target audience is a small subset of the paper's readership because the price is right¾free. For instance, if you are selling tax advice to wealthy individuals, don't hesitate to send news releases to the weekly papers that cover areas where these people live.

You might also be surprised at how little it costs to have a public relations writer put together a story for you. Many will work for $30 an hour or so, if they are independent and trying to build their business. The price is always very negotiable.

### 3. Conduct Seminars For Your Target Audiences

Large corporations offer free seminars to their prospects all the time. But there is no reason you can't do it on a local level also. By seminar I mean a one or two hour meeting that is informational and strictly "soft-sell" No overt sales pitches during the seminar. What you want to do is show your expertise. The sales will follow.

In promoting your seminar, the most important point to emphasize is the word "Free." The second most important point is "information." The third is "no obligation." Then all you have to do is provide free information with no obligation. You can send notices to your target list inviting them to the seminar or, if the number is small, have someone in your office invite them personally. You might even want to do this yourself.

Here are a couple ideas on how to do this on a small or non-existent budget. Since your seminar is free and educational, you can approach schools and churches to use one of their meeting rooms. A minimal donation would not be inappropriate. Don't worry about flashy handouts. Just put the information in easy to read form and it will be appreciated. Be sure your name and a phone number are prominently displayed so that people will be able to find you when they need you. And they will.

I have built my marketing communications practice largely through speaking to groups. I present 30-40 minutes of information similar to what is in this book to audiences ranging in size from 10 to 90 people. In many instances, people will come up to me at the conclusion of my presentation and ask me if I would be interested in working with their company. This has led to quite a bit of business. But a seminar doesn't stop selling at the conclusion of the presentation. Your handouts find their way into many businesses you would never otherwise visit. I've had numerous calls from people who have read my handouts and been attracted by the information in them.

Be careful how you evaluate your seminar. While working at Deloitte & Touche, I arranged for a seminar on pollution control credits for high tech manufacturing companies. Out of 100 individuals invited, only 4 attended. I was crestfallen at the time. But in talking to the individual who made the presentation, I found that those 4 people had bought over $30,000 worth of tax review and consultation time. The meeting room had cost $200 and the coffee and donuts another $50. Not a bad investment. Besides, I took most of the leftover donuts home and made a great impression with my children.

## 4. Become Recognized As an Expert in Your Field

I have always been of the opinion that in any industry built upon knowledge and expertise the best marketing strategy is to be recognized as the information leader. Companies do this by sharing their knowledge with others through printed publications and other media, increasingly the Internet. Small companies and even individual professionals and salespeople can do this also.

I recommend to my clients that they publish a quarterly newsletter that offers information that their prospective customers can use in their daily work or private lives. This helps to build the position that the company is the source of information in their business. I recently completed my first issue of new client newsletter in the insurance adjusting field. Two of the stories in that newsletter are instructional, in that they help insurance companies do a better job of handling claims. As the prospects read these stories, they gain an appreciation for my client's knowledge and expertise. Then, when an independent adjuster is required to handle a claim, my client is foremost in the insurance company executive's mind and the recipient of an urgent call.

You don't have to spend a lot of money to prepare such a newsletter, but make sure it is neat and well written. I have received a number of newsletters, the majority from real estate agents, that have been amateurish and counter-productive in building the agent's image. Be sure any information you convey is of appropriate quality for your audience. As Marshal McCluhan said in the '60s, "The Medium is the Message."

## 5. Court Influencers

These are individuals or companies who may not be your prospective customer but can influence your prospects' buying decisions. In the accounting field, bankers and lawyers are certainly influential in directing business to favored firms. In the advertising business, media salespeople are well known for their ability to influence advertisers' agency selections. In a more formal sense, a cadre of well-paid consultants influence how their clients spend money on everything from equipment to services in an every growing variety of businesses.

With their increasing clout, it would be a mistake to overlook influencers as sources, albeit indirect, of business. But how do you go about influencing the influencers?

The best way to gain the trust and approval of influencers is to do a great job for your present customers and then make sure the influencers in your market know about it. Remember what I said about using newsletters? If you develop a newsletter, make sure you distribute it to your influencers. Also, look for influencers in the organizations you support. And don't be afraid to tell them exactly what you want from them — leads on new business. It's definitely a "you support me and I'll support you" proposition.

Many of these type arrangements are being organized into lead clubs or similar groups. Non-competing salespeople from a variety of industries get together on a regular basis to exchange information about new business prospects in their areas. Although I haven't participated in one, I am told that they can be especially helpful in uncovering small business opportunities. However, the quality of the groups is totally dependent on the quality of the participants and their dedication to truly sharing information.

One of Deloitte & Touche's best salespeople relied upon a group of influencers he assembled in the Los Angeles area. They worked in the dynamic high tech field where businesses sprang up (and went down) at a dizzying pace. As a result of having the entire group on the lookout for new business, they were able to cover a very large market much more efficiently than they would have been able to otherwise.

## 6. Distribute Newsletters

As my consulting clients will tell you, I am a fervent believer in newsletters as a promotional medium. When I use the word newsletter, don't think in terms of homemade gossip sheets or thinly disguised sales flyers. A good newsletter can reinforce your positioning in the marketplace and help you distribute your expertise to a large audience of potential buyers.

And don't believe that newsletters are only for large companies. With desktop graphics technology available today, even an individual salesperson with a rudimentary knowledge of computers can prepare an excellent newsletter. Software programs offer templates to house your information and quick printers such as Kinko's can provide copies at very reasonable costs.

The key to a successful newsletter is providing information, not sales points. By showing your expertise and mastery of your market, you immediately inhabit a top of mind awareness among your targets. When the time comes to buy, you'll get the call. Better yet, include an offer for free information in your newsletter. You'll initiate a two-way dialogue and capture a valuable prospect name for further marketing activities.

### 7. Use The Internet

I would be remiss if I did not add my voice to the multitudes writing and speaking about the unlimited potential of marketing via the Internet. Let me just say that the same approach you use in newsletters is mainly applicable to your web site, unless you sell directly via the Internet. Provide timely information that reflects your expertise. Make it easy for people to respond to you and always attempt to gather identifying information about your visitors. For an idea of what I mean, take a look at www.introvertsales.com. There you'll find some articles I've written, some biographical information and how you can contact me.

If done well, all the above activities will bring potential customers to you or at least turn cold calls into warm calls. Your prospects will already know you, know that you have expertise they need and be expecting you to help them buy. The perfect combination for the introvert sales pro.

## Short Term

"But the kids need to eat this week," you say. They can't wait till next month or whenever the long-term activities produce results. So add to your long-term activities some actions that can produce results much more quickly.

## 1. Following up Leads

Over the course of my marketing career, no subject has been so universal as the question of how to handle and follow-up leads generated by various marketing communications tactics. Whether it be bingo cards (if you are not acquainted with these, they are cards that are inserted into trade magazines. The reader has only to circle the number of an ad or press release to obtain information from the advertising company. Most salespeople consider these worthless), e-mail, phone calls, personal letters or other means of communications, leads represent someone's interest in your product or service and their desire for further information.

In my experience, many salespeople miss valuable selling opportunities by not pursuing these leads more aggressively. There are two main reasons for this. First is the fact that historically companies have failed to qualify too many leads, passing them on to the sales force without attempting to ascertain if they are indeed prospects. I've heard story after story of salespeople who wasted valuable time calling someone who needed information on electric motors for his son's school project or who bought one or two motors a year for a small machine shop. These "war" stories quickly spread throughout the sales force and good leads were thrown out with the bad.

This attitude isn't confined to selling products. At my accounting firm, senior partners often dismissed people that would call for information about services if they didn't represent large firms. While I am not suggesting that such leads should have been pursued by senior management, they could have been handled by younger professionals just beginning to build their own portfolios of business.

The second reason that leads are overlooked as a source of new business is that many inquiries represent future purchases as opposed to more immediate sales. Anyone whose compensation is based on commissions or billable hours will naturally gravitate to the sales opportunity that represents the quickest return on an investment of valuable time.

So what is my solution to this problem? If you work for a large organization, familiarize yourself with the qualification criteria used by your marketing department. Tell them what works for you and emphasize your commitment to pursue qualified leads. If you work for a small organization or for yourself, decide what criteria you will use to decide whether to follow a lead and then be sure to keep score of how well these criteria cull the 'bad" leads from the good.

Secondly, commit to erring on the side of following too many leads. Often, what might appear to be a small opportunity at first glance, might hold great potential upon further inspection. And even if you contact someone who might not be a prospect at this point in their business lives, they might one day be in a position to be a very attractive prospect. Can you take the chance that you might be alienating a future business prospect? Make time in your busy day to follow-up leads if they meet the most basic criteria for your business.

## 2. Advertising

Advertising, whether in newspapers, magazines, on the Internet, on radio or on television, is a great way to develop leads and prospects. However, unless you own your company or work for a very small firm, you probably don't have a great deal of input into your company's advertising programs. But even if you aren't involved in the production and placement of ads, here are a few tips to help you assess your advertising programs and how they generate leads for you.

*A. Always give the reader an incentive to act.*

So much advertising is wasted because it doesn't motivate the reader and give him or her a reason to take action immediately by calling for more information, asking to see a salesperson, or, in some cases, call with an order. Smaller companies usually cannot afford to slowly build awareness through advertising. They need responses and leads on a timely basis in order to stay in business.

You give readers an incentive to act by offering time sensitive promotions such as "10% off until January 1" or "Free software to the first 100 in the store." Another way is to offer free information that the reader must call to obtain. Once the reader calls, they usually are interested and can be turned into a customer without too much effort.

*B. Make it easy to respond.*

In today's busy world, convenience rules. Therefore advertising must not only ask for a response, but make it easy to respond by including not only a phone number but perhaps an 800 number, a fax number and an Internet address. You can't afford to make it difficult for any portion of your readers to respond

*C. Stress features not benefits.*

I get tired of saying this but I still see laundry lists of products and services rather than true benefits in ads. Even with my own clients, it is sometimes a battle to concentrate on benefits and not list every conceivable product or service they offer their customers.

*D. Target your advertising.*

The days of mass media are definitely numbered if not already dead, even on a local basis. You have community newspapers, weeklies and "shoppers" in just about every locale. The electronic media are just as targetable today, what with cable and satellite TV plus radio stations for every conceivable demographic group. Be sure to find the best fit with your target audience that you described above in the section on targeting.

## E. Spend enough to be noticed.

I said earlier that there is a glut of advertising messages facing the average American. Getting your message through demands that potential prospects be exposed to your sales message time after time before it is noticed. If in retail selling the mantra is location, location, location, in advertising the mantra is repetition, repetition, repetition. To do that, you have to be prepared to spend enough money to match your competition at the very least.

---

### Introvert Alert

No matter what your involvement in developing advertising, try to be the person in your organization that responds to inquiries. It shouldn't be too difficult, because many of the more typical salespeople have either become cynical toward leads that didn't quickly become sales or they perceive themselves as "sales hunters" able to track down and kill their own prey. You on the other hand know that leads are like crops waiting to be harvested by the skilled farmer. You can use your introvert personality to answer the inquiry with knowledge and professionalism that will result in sales. Additionally, the stereotypical, aggressive sales personality can quickly turn off an inquirer who may be looking for information with which to make an informed decision, not the hard sell.

---

One more note on advertising, especially if you are a very small company or individual. When most people think of advertising, they think in terms of the advertising they see on television, hear on radio or read in daily newspapers or magazines. They know such advertising is extremely expensive and way beyond their budgets. But instead of dismissing any type of advertising as inappropriate for you or your business, be creative and find more affordable and personal forms of promoting your business.

For instance:

Why not sponsor a little league team? Most teams have banners that they display at their games. It's a small investment but it puts your name in front of potential customers. It also helps the community.

Our children's school has a newsletter that solicits sponsors each month. I'm sure many schools have such publications. Chambers of Commerce have newsletters that accept advertising, as do industry and trade groups. The cost is small but the potential payback is huge.

## 3. Direct Mail

Direct mail is a very cost-effective alternative to media advertising, especially for small businesses. The smaller the number of targets you want to address and the more precisely you can identify likely prospects, the more you should consider direct mail. One of the problems with direct mail is that because it is so easy to develop, much of it is simply garbage. I'm referring to the tons of direct mail that goes directly from the mail into the trash in so many homes and businesses. This garbage is so poorly executed that it gives well-thought-out and conceived direct mail a bad name.

Good direct mail follows many of the rules of good advertising as described above. It gives the reader an incentive to act immediately, it makes it easy to respond, it stresses benefits not features, it targets a particular audience and it demands enough of an investment to be read by the recipient. This last point simply means if you want to be noticed and read you must have your direct mail prepared professionally by experts. Homegrown direct mail pieces usually betray their ancestry.

The hardest part of designing direct mail is finding a benefit that grabs the reader in the few seconds most of allocate to deciding whether to open a mailing piece or ditch it. Just remember that the reader's attitude is always, "So what does this do for me?" Be sure your direct mail answers that question quickly and effectively.

The simplest and most direct form of direct mail is the letter. If you have at least passable writing skills you can put them to good use in creating introductory letters that you use to precede a face-to-face appointment. The letter should point out some of the benefits you offer and a short personal or company introduction. You should know enough about the company or individual to have a good idea what concerns they have and how your product or service answers those concerns, at least in a general way.

These type letters can have two purposes. The best result would be for the recipient to call you to say he or she is interested and would like to see you. A good letter can do this. If it presents benefits that are apparent to the reader, you would be surprised at the reaction you can get. Direct mail gurus can tell you exactly how many responses you can expect. Then it becomes a numbers game. If you send out enough letters you'll get enough responses to keep you busy while you use your other more long term lead generating techniques.

You can significantly increase your response by using a letter to offer information that is useful to the recipient. This ties into your introvert sales characteristic of being a product/service specialist. From their first encounter with you, your customers and prospects will know you are a knowledgeable, serious salesperson. Big companies do this on a large scale. You can do it on a personal scale whether you are a CPA firm, a software provider or insurance salesman. You have the knowledge, you have the power. Offer to send the recipient the information and then you have an opening to call and ask if he received the information, if it was helpful and if he has any additional questions. That follow-up call is not a cold call. It's not red hot, but it isn't cold, either.

## 4. Referrals

As most insurance salespeople can tell you, they began their careers by attempting to sell coverage to friends and family. When they ran out of these, their real sales careers began. The next step was asking these same friends and family for referrals. And so it is in any type sales. Referrals are a great way to build a business and warm up those dreaded cold calls. When you can open your conversation with something like, "John Smith gave me your name and said you may be interested in..." you give your listener a point of reference and bestow upon yourself at least some legitimacy in comparison to a total stranger. The referral should give you added confidence also because you have an opening line that is much superior to anything else you might be able to use.

When calling always make sure you use the name of your contact immediately and then get to the benefit your product or service offers.

In some case you might even be able to have your referral source call your prospect to alert them to your impending call. Obviously this is the best scenario for you. It might be awkward to ask someone to make such a call, but if it is offered be sure to enthusiastically accept the offer. If, as you hope, a referral leads to new business be sure to thank your source in whatever manner is appropriate for your circumstances. But never let a successful referral go without a sincere "thank you" in person and in writing.

## 5. Surveys

Here's an interesting way to open doors. If you have a number of target companies in an industry or offer a specific service to a number of prospects, try sending them a survey on their needs and concerns. Offer to share the results with them after compiling the responses. This is helpful in two ways. At minimum, it will give you insight into your prospect's needs and expectations. But it will also give you a reason for calling to make an appointment to share the results. If you cannot share the information in person, at least you have shown yourself to be a player in the market and you will be able to get your survey, and your name, in front of prospects.

Two keys to the success of a survey are taking the time to make the information relevant, not only to you, but also more importantly to your targets. The other is to insure that completing the survey is quick and easy. Nothing can insure a low response more than a long or complicated survey. The idea is to have someone complete it at first glance. If it finds its way to a pile on the recipient's desk it most likely will never be returned.

### 6. Cold Calls

We might as well face it. No book on selling would be complete without a chapter on that old bugaboo, cold call selling. I can think of no other selling subject that creates more dread in current and potential salespeople. It accounts for many leaving selling altogether and creates ill will toward salespeople. I think it also is a major difference between extroverts and introverts. Of course, being an extrovert is no guarantee that the person is good at cold call selling, but the people that I have met who have been good at cold calls have been extroverts exclusively. I think this is probably true on larger basis, also.

Before proceeding, let me say that I hate cold calls. I think they are a waste of time and effort. Before you dismiss my remarks, let me also say that I believe in some instances and with some people, cold call selling can be a successful part of a selling effort. But, to my mind, introverts have many other options that offer greater returns than beating your head against the wall, trying to be successful at cold calling.

What is a cold call? In my terms a cold call is an initial effort to reach someone by phone or in person with no prior contact, reference or other preparation. Any bit of connection can warm a call to some degree. For instance, knowing that someone may be in the market for your product or service makes a cold call warm. I acquired one of my biggest accounts like this. A division of a Fortune 500 company moved to St. Louis from the East Coast. An office products sales person told us that the division had moved and might be looking for a local advertising agency. I called, got an appointment and began work with a new client in a few weeks. To me, that was not a cold call. Cold calling was phoning companies that I didn't know were looking for an agency and didn't know my company. I didn't neglect them. I just initiated the relationship in a different manner.

I don't believe in cold calls in most selling situations. Here's why:

### A. You are interrupting busy people

If it seems everyone is busy today, it is because they probably are. What with downsizing, rightsizing or whatever word is being used this month, the survivors are working harder than ever. As a result, there's less time at home and even that time is just as harried as at work. Just look at the food industry where there is an almost constant parade of new convenience foods for eating on the run. It's a busy world out there. No time to fix dinner. No time to fix breakfast. Go. Go. Go. Do you think someone really can take the time to listen to your pitch? And in business situations, who wants to admit they have time to listen to unsolicited calls?

### B. You've Got to Make It Fast

Catching busy people is only half the battle. As a nation, we have the attention span of a 10-second sound bite. Unless you are selling something that can be grasped in 10 seconds or less, you'll have a tough time keeping your listener tuned into your message. Sales training books say you have to have your benefit in your first few words. That's tough on the phone when someone is disturbed in the middle of other pursuits.

### C. Equated with "telemarketing" scams

A recent NBC News report on home improvement scams advised viewers not to do business with contractors that call you, implying that companies that employ telemarketing are more apt to be crooked than other companies. That's a common perception, deserved or not. Anytime you employ telemarketing in pursuit of new customers, you equate yourself with telemarketers who have earned the negative distinction. Besides, who hasn't been interrupted in the middle of dinner with the dreaded, "Mr. Murphy do you own your home there in Beaverton?" Or, "Mr. Murphy you've won a free prize... (click)?

### D. Gatekeepers dedicated to preventing

In his book *Successful Cold Call Selling*, Lee Boyan gives a number of tips on how to get around so-called gatekeepers. He tells salespeople to simply push their way through to an executive either in person or on the phone. Good luck. I don't pretend to say this could never happen, but I think there are much better ways to spend your time.

### E. Associated with fast-talking old style salespeople

Even if you are selling Girl Scout cookies over the phone, you are being lumped in with siding, windshield replacement, resort property and magazine subscription telemarketers. Rightly or wrongly, those people have earned the enmity of Americans for their interruptions in our lives. Do want your company associated with what are perceived as less than honorable businesses. I don't think so. But that's what you are doing when you cold call.

*F. You are probably making yourself miserable!*

Even the best cold call salespeople admit to having problems making the dreaded calls at one time or another. The ones who have overcome their anxiety say that anyone can do it. Anyone can become a cold call expert if you just keep trying. I don't agree. I think it is a debilitating practice that simply turns off many people who would otherwise make great salespeople. For all the reasons cited above, cold call selling is a real negative.

Take a look at the ads for salespeople in a Sunday newspaper. Quite a few say "no cold calling." Others emphasize that leads will be provided. The people placing these ads must know that the thought of cold call selling is simply a terrible negative to a lot of salespeople.

Can sales be made through cold calls. Of course they can. I won't deny that. But it takes a special type of personality, one not usually associated with introverts. And it also takes certain products. Professional services are not among these.

The futility of cold calling was captured years ago by publisher McGraw Hill in a classic ad to promote the use of trade magazine advertising. In the ad, a very stern-looking curmudgeon stared out from the page while the copy down the left side of the page read something like this:

*I don't know you*
*I don't know your company*
*I don't know your customers*
*I don't know your reputation*
*Now what did you want to sell me?*

He would certainly scare most introverts and probably a lot of extroverts also. You can face such a situation either across a desk or on the phone. All the marketing communications tactics discussed above are designed to change some of that old man's views and help you to make a sale. Your chances of making a successful sale would be much better if he said:

*I know you*
*I know your company*
*I know your customers*
*I know your reputation*
*I'm interested in what you have to sell.*

At that point you can concentrate on showing your expertise and how your product/service will benefit him. Think for a minute about the difference in approach between facing your prospect with no preparation and facing him with the knowledge that he wants and needs to talk to you.

## Summary

A key ingredient of *Successful Selling for Introverts* is the use of marketing communications techniques to drive prospects to you, the salesperson. Whether you work for a large company, a small firm or have your own business, there is an appropriate communications medium that you can use to turn cold calls warm and entice individuals to identify themselves as prospects. Once you have a continuing flow of prospects interested in you and your products or services, you are well on your way to success.

Part 4

# The Introvert Salesperson in Action!

# Chapter 12

# Your WOW! Statement

H ave you ever met someone at a reception and inno-
cently asked, "So what do you do for a living?" and
they replied, "I'm heading a biotech company that
increases crop yields to feed the world's hungry, teaching a class
in entrepreneurship to underprivileged children and working
on my Ph.D. in applied physics." All you could say in answer
was "Wow!"

Now most of us don't have those kind of credentials, but I'm
sure we can develop a short, pithy statement that tells the listener about our business and what makes it special in 30 seconds or less. That's what a WOW statement is. Think of it as a
30 second commercial that puts your best foot forward and
makes your listener say, "Wow!

Unfortunately, most people never prepare a WOW statement.
They just wing it. When they are introduced to someone and
asked about their business pursuits, they give either a too short
or too long response. Usually, the introvert gives too short an
answer and the extrovert too long an answer. Let's look at some
typical replies given by a commercial photographer.

When asked what he does, Joe, the introvert photographer,
replies, "I'm a commercial photographer. I do weddings on the
weekends."

When asked what he does, Jack the extrovert photographer replies, "I'm a commercial photographer and I do weddings on the weekends. I can shoot anything there is. Just last week I shot a building opening. Do you use photography? Can I call you next week? I've done photography for a lot of people. You know Joe Jones, the developer? Personal friend of mine. I shoot all his buildings."

When asked what he does, Jim, the *Successful Selling for Introverts* seminar graduate says, "I'm a commercial photographer specializing in architectural photography used by developers to promote their properties. On the weekends I do wedding photography, especially outdoor ceremonies where I can take advantage of beautiful, natural settings."

Can you feel the difference in the three approaches? What kind of impression would each one make? I would think your reaction to Joe would be a simple, "That's nice." Your reaction to Jack might be to flee to another corner of the room. But Jim has given you enough information that you understand what it is he does and what is special about it. My guess is that you would continue your conversation with him and remember him after your initial meeting.

As you can see from Jim's response, in order to be effective a WOW statement must be enthusiastic, positive, customer-focused and factual. Let's take a look at each of these.

## Enthusiastic

Remember that your WOW statement is like a 30-second commercial-for you. Have you ever seen a commercial that wasn't enthusiastic? And if you aren't excited about your profession or business, how can you expect anyone else to be? You have to project your positive attitude toward your business to be most effective in any selling situation, but especially at your first contact with someone who might be a potential customer or, even more likely, might tell someone else about the enthusiastic person they met recently. Don't let this opportunity slip away.

If you are thinking that you have to be like Jack to be enthusiastic, don't worry. A smile, a firm handshake and a sense of confidence in what you do are all that's needed. Remember that you have your WOW statement at the ready. You should always be confident and never have to be at a loss for words.

## Positive

Being positive is closely related to being enthusiastic. You want to tell people what you do, not what you don't do. But in many instances people explain themselves in negative terms. What if your photographer said, "I do commercial photography, but not kids and families? I shoot buildings. On the weekends I shoot weddings, but only outside." Can you hear the negative tone in those type statements? Accentuate the positive at all times in telling people what you do and they will be more positive toward you.

## Customer Focused

Remember, I said in chapter two that every contact a potential customer has with you helps to create a favorable impression of you and your business. Just like any other contact, a WOW statement has to be benefit oriented, not feature oriented. The photographer takes architectural photos to help building owners sell buildings and concentrates on outdoor weddings where he can provide beautiful photos in natural settings. Those are benefits, not features. You can't expect your listener to match features and benefits. You have to do it for them quickly.

## Factual

This might seem self-evident, but when you look upon every use of your WOW statement as a sales opportunity, you approach it with the same dedication to truth as you would a formal sales call. After all, you expect to create a business opportunity from your contacts. You want to build those contacts on truth and trust. Boastfulness and downright untruthfulness could lead to great embarrassment down the road. Be proud of what you do, but make sure it is truthful and you can back up any statements you make.

---

*Introvert Alert*

Having a WOW Statement can be an introvert's greatest ally in a situation where you are meeting a number of new people. If you are not comfortable making small talk, your WOW statement will engross you in a conversation quickly. If it is compelling, your WOW statement will elicit questions from your listener and before you know it you're in the middle of a good networking opportunity. Being armed with your WOW statement makes networking opportunities a lot less stressful.

---

**Try It Yourself**

In the blank space below, write your personal WOW statement. Remember it must be between 15 and 30 seconds in length and accurately portray what's special about you or your business.

_____

_____

_____

_____

_____

Now try it out on family members, business associates and friends. Does it capture your essence? Does it accurately tell what's special about you? If they agree, it's time to try it out on a new contact. Practice it at home until you have it memorized and it sounds natural and confident. Then, the next time you attend a business or other social function, go for it. Listen for your contact's response. If they say, "WOW", that's great. But more likely you'll know you are on the right track if they ask questions about your business and seek more details. Then follow up with your business card and off you go.

By the way, here's my WOW statement: I am a writer and sales consultant dedicated to helping individuals who identify themselves as introverts to be successful sales people. I write books and articles, conduct seminars and consult with individuals and companies on how to maximize introverts' sales potential, especially in the professions.

## Summary

Having a WOW statement can take much of the nervousness and uncertainty out of meeting new people and prospects. It can increase your confidence and help you make the most out of the limited selling time most of us squeeze into our busy days. I use my web address as a kind of WOW statement also, www.introvertsales.com. I have had numerous business contacts outside of my consulting practice ask me the significance of the address and I answer with my WOW statement. Be sure to develop yours — and use it.

# Chapter 13

# The Initial Sales Call

At this point I am going to assume that you have read the section on Customer Information and have done your homework prior to calling on a new prospect. You know some basic information about the company, it's organization, markets, etc. In the course of your research you have confirmed that the company is a viable buyer of your product or service, and you know what you would like to have them buy from you.

You have an appointment with someone who seems to be at least an influencer if not the final buying authority for the product or service you represent. So what do you want to accomplish at this initial meeting? (I am assuming this is a business-to-business sales call that will most likely require a number of meetings before a sale is made.)

According to McGraw-Hill's Business Information Bureau, the cost of a business-to-business sales call averages $251.63, so it is important that you make the most of any selling opportunity. The best way to do this to be totally prepared by knowing what you want to accomplish during the sales call, how you will do it, and how you will measure your success. Write down your plan and be as specific as possible about your goals and the steps that will move your prospect through the buying process.

There should be three objectives to an initial sales call. They are, in order of importance:

1. Decide if you want this person or company as a customer.

2. Gather enough information with which to make a formal presentation/proposal.

3. Introduce your company and yourself.

---

### Introvert Alert

I confess. Smiling does not come naturally to me. In fact, I tend to appear rather pensive, deep in thought. I would venture to say that many introverts share this trait. If you have trouble smiling when meeting new people, you need to make a conscious effort to appear friendly and approachable. I've spent a long time trying to get over my habit of not smiling and today I make sure I face the world with at least a half-smile. I usually remind myself that this is only business, not a life or death situation, before approaching someone. It seems to work. Just be careful not to wear a forced smile or toothy grin. Practice in front of a mirror a few times until you see and feel your natural smile appear.

---

## Do You Want Them as a Customer?

At first, you might find this an odd question. Of course you want them as a customer if they are willing and able to pay, don't you? But look more closely. Many times an eager buyer can turn into a customer from hell. Depending on the product and its life cycle, you may want to be wary of prospects/customers that fit one of these descriptions:

*The Clingers.* They need so much service that you lose money working with them. Especially in the professions, these are the worst clients. In accounting, they are the ones that call every day with a new question that must be answered by a partner or other senior person. The staff accountant can't possibly know the answer. In other professions the "clingers" have continuing

112

changes to drawings or agreements and an endless barrage of "what-ifs" they expect to be answered for free.

"Clingers" are tough clients for the introvert sales person who prides himself or herself on providing great customer service. You're smart and your clients know it. They continually want to pick your brain at no charge to them. You can usually predict when a prospect will become a "clinger" by the endless questions during the selling process and the number of meetings required before they will make up their minds and hire you or buy your product.

I'm not suggesting that you totally avoid these types or run away at the first signs of their being "clingers." But just be aware of what you are getting into and build some defenses into your proposals. You might put a cap on "free" consultations or make sure any changes to plans or contracts include the opportunity for you to be paid for any extra time needed to satisfy their demands.

*Price Questioners.* These type clients were(are) the bane of the advertising business. These are the clients who approve the $20,000 ad production invoice but want to know who made the $2.50 long distance phone call you are passing on to them at cost. They study every invoice hoping to catch you in a $5.00 overcharge. Every profession or industry has these suspicious customers.

Of course, clients have the right and obligation to be sure they are getting their money's worth, but the "price questioner" makes you feel as if he or she suspects you of stealing from them every time you submit an invoice. As a result, you can spend an inordinate amount of time substantiating every nickel of every invoice and less time solving the customer's problems.

You can spot these potential clients by their questions during the interview process. I actually had one prospect ask me if my advertising agency had a price list, as if we were a fast-food drive-in. You can't really win in that case. You get a new account and everyone is happy, but then as every charge is challenged you find you can't make any money. Your time is spent on an account that provides no profit to you and keeps you from pursuing more valuable clients.

Over time, a good salesperson can overcome this suspicious attitude. It takes patience and, often, a thick skin. If you are honest and open with your clients, they will react positively to your sincerity. I always told my clients that I personally stood behind every one of my agency's invoices. And I did. Nothing went out until I had seen it and approved it. That way I was sure my clients were being treated fairly. They appreciated it.

But before you take on a "price questioner" client be sure you are prepared to defend every invoice and justify your profit. Then make an informed decision if you want this client.

---

### Introvert Alert

Having "good clients" is more important to introverts because of the close relationships we tend to build with our clients. We want to feel that we are part of the team and are dedicated to helping further our clients' goals and objectives. Clients that keep us at arm's length for any reason can keep us from being our best for them.

---

*The Shoppers.* These are the clients that just want a bit of your knowledge. They're not interested in a relationship, but just a quick transfer of your knowledge — to them.

In the advertising business "shoppers" wanted to pick and choose a service or project for you to work on and then look for another "vendor" for the next job. In accounting, they may give your the audit, but "shop" every consulting project to other firms. They are the types that use the word "vendor."

As an introvert salesperson, this is not a win-win situation for you. You never have the opportunity to use your strengths, i.e., building rapport and showing your extensive knowledge. Leave the 'shoppers" to the extroverts that are more adept at shorter relationships. Thankfully, as we discussed, the business world is moving away from these types of arrangements and focusing more on lasting relationships that are mutually beneficial. Companies are coming to value the kind of selling that puts a premium on introvert-style relationships.

Am I saying that if your prospect shows any of the above characteristics you should not sell them? No, I am not. But if you are selling a professional service or some other kind of product that requires an on-going relationship, be aware of the pitfalls that await you from the very beginning.

I know a free-lance graphic artist that is always complaining about her clients. One is always making changes to materials that have already been approved, another won't pay for all the marketing guidance she gives them and the third wants just graphic ideas that an in-house artist will execute, usually to the detriment of the original concept. When I ask her why she puts up with these "bad" clients she says she needs the money. But because of all the time it takes to satisfy these "bad" clients, she really isn't making that much money. Plus, she's too busy to find "good" clients.

The moral of the story is: "pick your clients well."

*The Stone Walls.* Finally, there are some prospects with whom you just don't get along. You can feel it from the first time you meet. You don't like them and they don't like you. Before all the sales managers attack me, let me say that the best way to handle this situation is to pass the account off to a colleague if at all possible. This isn't being a quitter. If you feel strongly that you don't like this person, they probably feel it too. Cut your losses and get a different player into the game. Don't butt your head against the wall.

I once called on a general manager of a marking products company. A former co-worker of mine had gone to work for the company as a marketing manager and wanted me to do some communications work for his new company. But first I would have to pass muster with the general manager.

The GM was a hulking, jowly man who spoke very broken English. He actually met me in the lobby of his offices and, to my surprise, quickly sat down next to me and opened the conversation with, "So, what you got."

I started to give him some background on my agency and why I was visiting with him, but he kept interrupting to make remarks such as "advertising agencies cost too much" or "What do you know about my business?" I couldn't get a full sentence in.

Then he looked out the front window at my car parked immediately in front of the door. "Is that your car?" he began. I replied that it was mine. "I knew it," he continued. "You charge too much so you can pay for that car."

That was it for me. That car was a 1982 Saab (this was 1989) and it was bleeding me dry between repairs and gas. So I politely told him that my car was none of his business and that I didn't care who he used for his marketing work. It wouldn't be me.

Can you imagine what he would have been like as a client? Sorry, I don't agree with anyone who says every sale is worth the price. As an introvert, it is very hard to be phony and hide my feelings. So I don't try. If I had been selling a machine that was a one-time purchase and didn't require an on-going relationship, I would have been willing to accept the general manager's attitude. But not in the situation before me.

Another important consideration is whether your prospect can afford your product or service. As a marketing manager in a Big 6 (at the time) accounting firm, this was a continual question. Many younger accountants spent too much time pursuing smaller clients that clearly could not and would not pay the hourly fees associated with such a large firm. We had big corporate clients and our pricing structure reflected it. Many were public companies that needed the prestige of a large firm to attract capital and were willing to pay for it.

Selling someone a product or service that is clearly not appropriate for them is no way to build a long-term relationship whether in business-to-business selling or in consumer selling. The way to make a customer for life is to solve the customer's problem at a price they can afford. Car companies were built on this concept. Sell the right person the right car at the right time and they will stay with you as their needs and ability to pay changes. The young man buying the Escort will someday buy the Windstar van for his young family and the Lincoln to show his success later in life.

---

*Introvert Alert*

By being more concerned about your buyer's need for value rather than your need for the biggest possible sale, you'll help build trust and gain positive referrals from your satisfied customers.

---

As strange as it may seem, the decision to accept someone as a customer is crucial for your ultimate success. A large amount of business with the wrong clients can make you very successful for a short period of time. Good clients can keep you successful for a long time. So choose them well.

## Information Gathering

The second task of any initial sales call is to gather enough critical information with which to make a presentation or proposal. For many salespeople this is a crucial step that can mean success or failure with a new prospect. Only by uncovering real needs can you hope to fulfill those needs with your product or service. Too often, salespeople walk away from an initial meeting with little information and then make a garden-variety proposal based upon the product features in general or the salesperson's perception of the prospect's needs.

The exploratory conversation is where the introvert can shine.

Because you've done your homework, you don't spend time asking basic questions. You know the company. You know its markets and industries. Your questions will help to reveal to the contact that you are a serious professional armed with information. You know what information you need to get out of this meeting and you'll make sure you get it.

Here are six basic questions that will get the answers you need. Of course you will have to adapt them to your particular product or service.

1. What's your present situation in regards to my product or service?

2. Is that situation satisfactory to you and your company?

3. If it isn't, how would you like to see your situation changed and how long do you want it to take?

4. What do you think will be your biggest challenges in meeting your objective?

5. What role do you see (your product or service) playing in changing this situation?

6. How are you going to judge the contribution my product or service makes to your success?

To further illustrate what I mean by the above question, here are some answers that could be provided by a prospect for a direct mail campaign:

1. We want to sell books on the history of people named Murphy in the United States. We think direct mail might be a way to do it, but we don't know how to go about putting together a program to reach these people.

2. We need to get this done because it presents a great opportunity for us to increase our profits from selling these type books.

3. We want to sell 10,000 books over the next six months and need a program that can help us do it.

118

4. It seems there are a couple of big hurdles. How do we find all the people named Murphy and then how do we put together a compelling mailing piece that will sell our books?

5. We need a plan to get the mailing list at a reasonable cost, in the format needed for mailing and then an inexpensive mailing piece. We need it to make our profit projections for the next six months.

6. A successful program should help us move 10,000 books and we expect most of that to come from the direct mail campaign, so it has to be hard-hitting.

If you can leave an initial meeting with answers like these to those six basic questions, you should be able to present a solution that will meet your customer's needs and that he will pay for.

The biggest pitfall in an initial meeting is that you will tell your contact everything about your company, product, history, experience, offices, other clients and organizational structure and not find out much about their company. Then you go back to your office and prepare a presentation to tell them more about your company and your experience.

Naturally, you need to establish your credentials at your first meeting. But it should be done economically and mainly through anecdotes about how you have helped other companies. In describing my agency, rather than saying we had 30 years experience in direct mail with over 40 clients, I would always try to give concrete examples of how we helped other companies, e.g., "we recently developed 400 leads for one of our clients and 40 became customers, providing a 500 per cent return on their investment." Or "we developed a direct mail campaign that offered cream pies to our client's customers if they met with a salesperson. We had 23 out of 45 invite the salesmen in and 18 bought."

These examples show you know the business, care about results and could do the same thing for the listener.

*A couple more ideas:*

Have a written plan for your meeting, including the questions you would like to have answered. This will help you direct the meeting back on course when it inevitably strays to other subjects and will remind you of the information you need to have before the end of the meeting. Just a few minutes thinking about what you specifically want to accomplish can pay great dividends. In the course of your pre-meeting research a number of possible questions should come to mind. Jot those down and be prepared.

Of course you should always take extensive notes during your meetings. As a courtesy, I always ask if my prospect minds if I take notes and then try to capture as much on paper as possible without losing the flow of the conversation. Close listening is important and with experience you can listen and write at the same time.

Always ask for clarification if something is not clear to you. This can be a real positive in many ways. Obviously it can make clear what is unclear or what you don't understand, but it can also be a sign of the importance you are placing on the speaker's words. I am not speaking of questioning facts or opinions at this point. But I want you to be sure you completely understand the speaker's words and concepts before moving on to other subjects. An example of such a clarification question would be, "You say you want to increase your market share. Could you expand on how you plan to do that?"

The above is an open-ended question that invites the speaker to provide lengthy information. Closed-end questions are ones that can be answered with a yes or no, or with one or two words. In the above example, the closed-end versions would have been, "You say you want to increase market share. Are you going to do it through capturing competitor's share or growing the market?" The answer, "capturing share from competitors," gives you some information but not as much as the open-end version will elicit.

There are many books specifically on questioning techniques. The successful introvert salesperson will study them and develop his or her own process for getting information during the course of meetings.

## Introduce Your Company and Yourself

This subject is usually thought of as the main objective for the initial sales call. For the Sales Hunter this may be true. But remember we are Sales Farmers harvesting the fruits of our labor.

As I explained earlier, in its most basic form, the sales process involves four steps: Awareness, Interest, Desire and Action. It is the job of Marketing and Sales people to move a prospect along this path as quickly as possible. As you remember, the Sales Hunter takes on this entire burden from making initial contact (awareness) to the close (action). The Sales Farmer uses marketing communications tactics to accomplish awareness and interest, and then harvests sales through building desire and asking for action. As a result, in most instances the Sales Farmer does not need to use precious face-to-face selling time with a prospect to introduce the company. He or she can move directly to the desire stage.

Too many sales people turn their initial meeting with a prospect into a long introduction of their company. They drone on about the company history, the seasoned veterans that make up the staff and their complete dedication to quality and service. Many have meticulously prepared their "pitch" and it sounds like it.

I have always preferred to let written material convey that type information. Formal flyers or pages prepared especially for the meeting can recite credentials and customer lists.

*Introvert Alert*

If you are feeling uneasy about making a sales call, be careful not to slip into the "canned" presentation trap. That's where you memorize what you think are important facts and figures about your company and product, and then launch into a recitation of your "pitch" without first becoming acquainted with your listeners and their situations. Such presentations usually sound "phony" and never help to build a relationship between you and your prospect.

## Summary

The first sales call on a prospect is an opportunity for both you and the prospect to answer some basic questions about the other. Many a salesperson has rued the day they began working with the "client from hell." The more contact you have with a client, the more important it becomes to be compatible at some level. The best way to insure that you make a considered decision on accepting a new customer or client is to have a list of questions you want answered during your initial meeting. Do your preparation before the meeting and you'll be more likely to accomplish your objectives while in front of your prospect. Hopefully, you will leave your initial meeting with a sale or at least the knowledge that your buyer is a person with whom you can work and develop a relationship. And remember; never leave a meeting without a reason to get back in touch with your prospect with additional information.

# Chapter 14

# Answering Questions

For many of us, the thought of having to hear and respond to a tough question or objection can be a major hurdle to overcome. Sure, we can present our sales message, remember all the salient points, give the technical details of our product or service, and proceed smoothly on our way to the sale. No problem.

But then our listener takes issue with one of our points, asking questions or making statements such as, "How do you know this? What guarantee is there that this will work? I don't agree." That's when we either become real salespeople or simply skulk away without a sale. After all, if everyone were eager to buy in the first place, there wouldn't be a need for salespeople, would there?

Nevertheless, we worry that we may not have the correct answer immediately. We worry about giving an incorrect or incomplete answer. We fear that an objection is a personal rejection and avoid addressing it head-on, hoping it will go away.

But, if selling is to be a part of success in your profession, you will eventually need to address the issue of objections head-on and accept the fact that your prospects will inevitably take issue with you and will not always accept your word as gospel.

You'll have to persuade them that your view is correct and

that what you say is true. That's not always easy, but thankfully, there are ways to prepare for objections and be ready to answer them. And, as you've learned throughout this book, there are approaches that can be in tune with your personality and reflect your concern for your customers and their needs.

Once again, I disagree with most sales training books that spend a considerable amount of time talking about "Overcoming Objections." To me, that sounds like the predatory jargon so prevalent in old-style selling. I prefer to use the words, "Answering Objections and Questions." Doesn't that sound much more in keeping with the consultative tone we are trying to establish? "Overcome" sounds as if you are prepared to strong-arm them if they don't agree with you. How would you feel if your legitimate concerns and questions were viewed as obstacles to be overcome by some "Sales Rambo?"

By using the word "answering," salespeople are internally legitimizing the objection and the listener's right to have an opinion contrary to their own. Objections and questions arise from the listener's unique experience, value systems and perceptions. Once that is recognized and established, salespeople and prospects can work together to find an appropriate answer and continue on the road to fulfilling the prospects' needs and making the sale.

I've included both questions and objections in this chapter because I view objections as really a form of questioning. When a prospect raises the objection that "I want to think about it" they are really asking the question, "Why should I make this decision today?"

### Four Steps to Answering Questions and Objections

1. Prepare

2. Acknowledge

3. Answer

4. Move on

## Preparing for Questions and Objections

Have you ever been in the midst of preparing a sales presentation and a voice within you keeps asking, "What do you mean? How can this be? Are you sure?" This inner voice can be your best guide to the questions and objections that others will have upon hearing your presentation. Develop a talent for critically critiquing your presentations and answering questions raised by this inner voice.

Always answer your questions in a positive manner. For instance, if your inner voice asks, "Are we really going to turn this project around in five days?" be sure to include details on your staffing and delivery plans that will make it happen. Don't leave the question to be asked by your prospect. If your inner voice says, "How do I know they won't give us a low initial price and then raise prices later?" you can offer a guaranteed price for a set amount of time. Just build the answers to your questions into your presentation in positive, customer-friendly terms.

Once you have satisfied your inner voice and feel confident in your answers, you are ready to let your colleagues challenge you. As you practice your sales presentation (you are practicing, aren't you?), ask a fellow worker, friend or family member to listen to you and ask any questions that occur to them. When you are finished, ask if they would buy your product or service based upon the presentation. This can be a valuable lesson in dealing with questions and objections. Treat their comments seriously and try to answer them as completely as possible. Think of this exercise in terms of baseball's spring training. Get it right now, when it doesn't count, and you'll be prepared to win when the real season begins.

As you may recall, much of my sales experience was in the advertising agency business where you have the opportunity to make a great number of presentations, to individuals as well as groups. As a result, my colleagues and I knew that our ability to answer questions and objections was critical. To fine-tune our presentations, we would include as many people as possible in our "run-throughs." Attendees were encouraged to ask questions, point out inconsistencies and generally act like prospective clients. We all took our roles seriously, and as a result, some of these events could be rather heated. But that was good, because it prepared us for the worst possible scenarios. You don't want people who just sit and listen at these practice sessions. You want people who share their opinions and concerns.

Another way to prepare for questions and objections is to simply compare notes with others that have sales responsibility in your organization. During the course of my career, I have rarely seen a formal FAQ (Frequently Asked Questions) or FRO (Frequently Raised Objections) program. I would encourage anyone who sells as part of his or her profession to keep a notebook with this information handy. It will be a great help in preparing presentations that answer FAQs and FROs before your listeners can raise them. It also becomes a valuable tool in training people new to sales in your organization.

After you have listened to your inner voice, asked colleagues to critique you, and compared notes with others in your organization, you are ready for the big show. The good news is that after doing all the above, you are well prepared. The bad news is that it is very unlikely you will deliver a sales message or presentation without encountering at least some questions or objections. That's because you are dealing with human beings that bring their unique selves to your presentation. You can't hope to address each and every one of their special perspectives. With hard work and preparation you can identify the most common comments, but the odds are someone will have a slightly different opinion and often "come out of left field" with an objection. So now let's turn to how we deal with unforeseen questions or objections during your presentation.

---

*Introvert Alert*

If you have limited experience answering objections or you read many of the sales training books on the market, you might think the way to answer objections is to memorize trite phrases or turn a quick verbal slight of hand. That's not true. The best and most appreciated response is sincerity and honesty. That doesn't absolve you from the need to produce an answer, but it should tell you that you have the basic skill-you just need to practice it.

---

## Acknowledging Questions and Objections

The first thing you must do after a question or objection has been raised is to acknowledge the speaker and let them know you intend to address the issue. Besides being polite, these few moments will give you time to begin to formulate your response. Some common acknowledgments are:

*That's a good question.*

*I'm glad you brought that up.*

*Others have asked about that before.*

*Thank you for the opportunity to cover this in more detail.*

If you feel comfortable doing it, you can add some self-deprecating humor to your acknowledgment. Something like:

*I knew someone would catch me.*

*I can't get anything by you, can I?*

Just be careful to know your listener(s) before you attempt any humor. To the wrong audience it can be a killer.

After acknowledging the question, repeat it in your own words. This will tell the person that you understand the question and clear any misunderstanding before it goes any further. Of course, it also gives you even more time to develop your reply. You can begin to repeat the question with words such as:

*If I understand you correctly...*

*I'm hearing you say...*

During this time be sure to continue eye contact with your listener. Avoiding eye contact by looking away creates a subtle doubt that you are being sincere and honest, and are comfortable with the situation. Conversely, looking directly at the person builds trust and confidence in you.

At this stage, there are a number of pitfalls to avoid if you are to be successful. Don't become defensive when confronted with an objection or question, no matter how hostile or antagonistic these might sound to you. If you have prepared well and know your subject, there is no need to be defensive. The best defense is a wide smile and a polite "thank you" as you proceed to answer.

Also, be careful not to knock the competition, even when faced with untrue accusations. This happened to me once in the middle of a major presentation when our prospect said, "We hear you are very expensive and charge more than other agencies for the same work." Well, I knew where that comment originated because our chief competitor had been knocking us all over town with that inaccurate information. But instead of reacting instinctively, calling it a lie and sinking to the level of my competitor, I said that our current clients would tell him otherwise. I invited him to personally contact each one for their opinion about our billing rates. Of course, it wasn't possible to "prove" our rates were fair right there during our presentation, but by being open and honest and offering corroboration, the questioner was silenced and the issue diffused.

Sometimes, for whatever reason, your prospect, or individuals in a group presentation, will be critical of you and make untrue or unfair comments as part of their question or objection. This can be a very difficult situation, especially for introverts who are uncomfortable in a confrontational situation. While it may be true that some people do enjoy such confrontations and in fact may actually judge others by how well they fight back, most people will avoid such situations.

I worked for an agency owner who was an expert at dealing with clients (mostly in the retail and automobile businesses) who would scream (literally) at him and then turn around and hire him. With his soul mates he was great — giving as much as he took-but his style was offensive to many others, especially in the corporate world where a premium is placed on congeniality and teamwork.

As usual, I advise introverts to play to your strength. That is, don't get into arguments, even with people who may enjoy it. Rely upon your knowledge and keep your professional demeanor. Remember that most people don't like such confrontation. Avoid telling prospects and customers they are wrong. Never argue or accuse. It's just good business.

## Answering Objections

As I said, objections and questions are as numerous as the number of people you'll encounter. I can't give you an answer to every question, but here are some strategies to employ in addressing important issues:

*Proof.* The best answer is always to provide some sort of proof to your statements. If practical, it is preferable to include this proof as part of your presentation, but because of time constraints you can't always do this. But have the information ready, in case you need it. Proof can be physical, the exact reference information you used or corroboration by third parties.

*Explanation.* All too often, objections arise from a lack of understanding of your proposal or presentation. Being sure not to offend your listener, offer to go through an explanation again. Pause often to insure understanding of each critical aspect of your clarification. You may have moved too quickly during your initial presentation and lost your listeners along the way. Now you have the opportunity to clearly make your points.

*Flip Side.* This is a useful technique for turning problems into benefits. It works like this: A listener brings up a question or objection such as, "Why should a small company like mine, work with a big company like yours? I'll be overlooked as you take care of your bigger clients."

Taking the flip side, your answer might be something similar to: "That's a good question. In fact, we work well with dynamic, growing smaller companies That energizes our staff because it gives us an opportunity to show how we can help you grow and be part of your success. Working with larger clients helps us to understand the challenges you'll face as you grow. Plus, we'll have the resources to be your partner today and tomorrow. You won't outgrow us."

Do you see how the question of being too big has been turned around, how the potential problem of being too big has been turned into a benefit? That can be very effective. In fact, in certain situations, you might want purposely not to address an often asked question as part of your presentation but wait for it to come up and then make a powerful point with your prepared answer.

The most vexing of objections are those in the form of a statement. They are difficult to address for most of us. Sales training books usually provide answers in the form of "one-size fits all" tactics that, to me, seem manipulative and designed to "overcome" rather than address serious problems. I think most introverts are smart enough to develop their own strategies for dealing with these objections and offering answers that fit their own personalities and styles.

Following are some of the most common statement objections, and space to write responses that work for you. Give each answer serious thought before writing. To help you, I'll provide a clue to a good answer. But remember the best answer is the one that works for you, the one you can deliver honestly and sincerely. After you prepare your answers, try them out on colleagues and friends. Then, when you are faced with these statements while selling, you will have a comfortable, workable answer at the ready.

I don't have any money/budget for that.
*(break costs down into monthly, daily amounts; alternative financing solutions)*

_____

_____

_____

_____

We already work with a competitor.
*(Find out what's good about supplier then ask what could be improved, offer free trial)*

_____

_____

_____

_____

I want to think about it.
*(Look for hidden problems, provide additional support)*

_____

_____

_____

_____

We don't have a need now.
*(Discuss cost of not acting, find best purchase time, and keep in touch)*

_____

_____

_____

_____

Your price is too high.
*(Show value, life cost, added benefits)*

_____

_____

_____

_____

We'll get back to you.
*(Find reason to contact again)*

_____

_____

_____

_____

## Moving On

After you have answered an objection/question to the best of your ability, it is time to move forward in your presentation toward the point of asking for action, for a commitment. Just be sure you have answered the questioner to the best of your ability at that time. Always formally ask if you have covered the subject and if there are any lingering questions. Don't leave questions hanging in the air. They will hurt you later.

Of course, there will be occasions when you simply cannot completely answer a question or objection. In that case, promise to provide the information as quickly as possible. Be specific about your plans to reply and you will be believed. Think of it as another opportunity to contact the prospect and make a positive impression. It can show your prospect that you keep your promises and what they can expect when they become your client.

On the other hand, there will be instance when you must "agree to disagree" with a prospect or customer. Don't let it ruin your presentation. Acknowledge the difference of opinion and move to a positive point quickly.

If you approach questions and objections openly and sincerely, you will favorably impress your listeners and lead naturally to your request for action. As we will see in the next chapter, asking for a commitment is much easier if the road to action is paved with care and planning. You won't need 25 "can't miss" closes out of a book. The question of action will flow naturally as your prospect sees the advantages of working with you.

## Summary

Answering questions and objections need not be a problem for the successful introvert sales person. By preparing to deal with inevitable questions and objections, acknowledging them sincerely and answering them honestly, you will move swiftly through this stage to the actual commitment to action. Rather than fearing contrary opinions, you can use questions and objections to build your prospect's trust in you and make the ultimate sale even easier.

# Chapter 15

# Asking for a Commitment

No matter how well you use marketing tactics to moti
vate prospects to call you; no matter how well you know
your product or service; no matter how well you ask
questions and show concern; absolutely nothing happens until
you directly ask for a commitment from your prospective customer. This is the moment that brings fear to the feint-hearted,
be they introvert or extrovert.

As I've said before in this book, I detest the word close for
most selling situations. My preference for using "asking for a
commitment" instead of closing is much more than mere se-
mantics. Commitment implies an understanding of the sales
message and an agreement that the product or service is indeed
a solution to the buyer's problem or a positive contribution to
that person's personal or business life. It isn't a close; it is an
opening of a relationship with responsibilities and expectations.
Close would be more appropriate when a sale is not made.

But whether you call it a close or asking for a commitment, a
sale is rarely consummated without the salesperson directly asking for the business. I heard a story recently that shows the absolute necessity of asking for the sale.

A real estate agent was working late one night in his office
when he received a phone call from an individual who wanted

to make an offer on a home that was listed with the agent. The prospective buyer evidently knew the house, because he described it to the agent in glowing terms and said that it was the perfect house for him and his wife. The agent asked if he wanted to see the house before making an offer. But the man on the phone had seen the house, knew the asking price and was ready to make an offer. The agent asked the caller when he had seen the house and if he had an agent. The prospective buyer said that he had an agent who showed him the house and gave him all the details. Puzzled, the agent asked why he didn't buy the house when he first saw it. The answer was, "my agent never asked me to buy it."

I believe that type scenario is all too common in many sales situations. It's not surprising because the moment you ask for a commitment, you are asking for approval of everything you have done till that moment. In professional services, you are asking for even more. You are asking for validation of your abilities and your credentials to deliver your services.

---

*Introvert Alert*

Believe it or not, asking for a commitment can be the easiest part of selling for introverts. If you are selling a product or service you truly believe in and understand, it should not be difficult to honestly and forthrightly tell your prospective buyer that you feel what you have to offer will benefit him or her and deliver the promised benefit. A simple, "Don't you agree?" will communicate that now is the time for a commitment. When they agree, follow up with "When can we get started?" Practice this approach and it will become second nature. The key is to sell yourself to yourself first. Selling others is then the easy part.

---

So how do you know when a prospect is ready to make a commitment? There are five sure-fire signs that your prospects are close to making a decision and it is time for you to ask for the commitment:

The prospect asks about payment terms

The prospect asks when you could begin work or deliver products

The prospect speaks negatively about current suppliers

The prospect provides proprietary information

Prospects want to meet others in your organization who will be working on their business

There are two typical situations in which most of us ask for a commitment. In some instances, the listener can actually make a decision on the spot, accepting or rejecting your offer. You then have an opportunity to offer additional information or answer any objections. In other situations, primarily when you make a presentation to a group or as one of a number of potential service or product suppliers, you won't receive an immediate response to your request. The two should be approached somewhat differently.

## How to Ask for a Commitment When You Expect an Immediate Response

I believe much of the fear of asking for a commitment comes from the legacy of past sales training techniques. To me it always seemed that to be successful you needed to be like a card shark, shuffling the deck, looking for just the right "close" that would surprise the hapless prospect into surrendering and signing a contract out of fear or subterfuge. You know it doesn't have to be that way. If you subscribe to everything in this book so far, it would be ludicrous to now change into a winking, sleight-of-hand "closer." Many people still think that is a prerequisite for finalizing sales. It is not.

Asking for a commitment should be a natural progression based upon everything that you have said and done since your first direct contact with your prospect. If you have been a consultant-type sales person you don't have to give that up now. If you have created a win-win situation, don't try to overcome your prospect now. Take them along with you.

Ask if there are any more questions and if they fully understand your offer or proposal. At that point a question such as, "Does this make sense to you?" will subtly move the conversation toward a resolution.

Now is the time to make it easy for your new customer to feel comfortable. Be ready to set up the first working meeting, if that is required. If you have a contract, have it available to sign at that point. Always have the next step in mind for when your prospect becomes your customer. Know delivery dates. Know your schedule. Make them feel proud to have you on their team and vice versa.

Most important are a sincere "thank you" and a firm handshake. One more thing. Although I'm sure you have been enthusiastic during your entire sales process, it is now even more important that you be enthusiastic and genuinely excited. The customer may be nervous or fearful, but you can sweep them up in your enthusiasm and help them conquer any reservations by the simple excitement you generate.

## How to Ask for a Commitment in a Presentation

In the advertising agency business, we usually made a formal presentation to a group of people. The appointment of a new agency was not decided in the meeting, but was finalized at a private session following presentations by two or three candidates. Most professional services accounts are assigned like this. Asking for a commitment is much different when you don't expect an immediate answer.

Usually we had done extensive research in order to make a credible presentation. We would end the formal presentation with words similar to: "This presentation has given you just a glimpse of the dedication and intelligence we will bring to working with you. We are ready to go to work for you today. In fact, as you can tell, we have already begun to work for you in developing this presentation. Just give us the word and we'll jump into action."

You need to adjust the wording so it is appropriate for your industry, but the sentiments are similar. Be presumptive. For that moment, project your feeling that you are the winner and your prospect's deliberations will be nothing more than a rubber stamp. Show your enthusiasm and excitement. Don't show any reservations or self-doubt. Confidence can be highly contagious.

Your work isn't over at this point. After making a presentation most people will go back to their offices and write a thank you letter that will add absolutely nothing to their prospects for winning. Always use the after-presentation letter to reinforce your main points and add more compelling reasons for your assignment. This is the opportunity to clear up any questions or make up for any misstatements made during your presentation. You can even suggest the next meeting time to further reinforce the confidence you showed earlier.

### Summary

Asking for a commitment can be an easy, comfortable culmination to a successful sales call or presentation. In the best of cases, it should flow naturally as a result of the knowledge, concern for your prospects and solution orientation you have shown throughout your contact with a prospect. You don't change your course in mid-stream. Just be sure you give your prospect the opportunity to become your customer.

Not everyone will agree with you and buy when you desire. But you'll find a greater percentage will buy when you present your genuine self. The introvert sales person who is a sales farmer will find harvesting sales is enjoyable and doesn't create stress.

# Chapter 16

# Retaining Existing Clients

Working with existing customers is the most introvert-friendly aspect of selling. You've made contact. You've made your presentation and been accepted. Your customers know you and can appreciate the fact that you are a professional, dedicated to fulfilling their needs. You and your company are now part of the customer's team. But this is no time for complacency — quite the contrary. Working with your present clients can be a minefield of missed opportunities, unfulfilled expectations and shattered illusions. It takes hard work and attention to detail to retain your customers and clients, no matter what your business or profession.

Let's examine some of the practices that will keep your present customers satisfied and then review tips on increasing business with them.

## Be Totally Responsible

The first rule of account service is to be totally responsible for all aspects of your company's relationship with your customers. It is the only way to build a strong foundation that will endure the inevitable problems that are part of any business relationship. No one really expects business to be totally problem-free. But they do expect to have problems or concerns addressed honestly and quickly — by you, the salesperson. They don't want excuses or explanations, just solutions. Total honesty is the only alternative in these situations. If you don't have an answer at the time you talk to your client, let them know how you intend to get an answer. "I don't know" is not acceptable. More appropriate is, "I don't have all the details at this point, but we are meeting at 10 a.m. tomorrow with engineering and manufacturing to review the problem. I'll call you at 11." Just make sure you do call with an answer.

If at all possible, inform your customers of any problem before they find out on their own. Surprise is the enemy. When you are alerted to a difficulty, find a solution and call your clients as soon as possible with notification of the problem and the solution.

In the advertising agency business, we were constantly at the mercy of printers and magazine publishers. A client would direct us to place an ad in a magazine and expect to see the ad when promised. But from time to time something went awry or someone made a mistake. This is how I handled one such situation.

My client was introducing a new product and we placed an ad in the March issue of the leading publication in that market. As the account executive for this client, I had overseen the ad creation and gained approval of the media schedule. I signed off on the insertion order and checked to insure that the ad materials were sent to the publisher on time. But when I received my advance copy of the magazine, my client's ad was nowhere to be seen. I quickly called the magazine and had my sales representative tracked down. When he got back to me, the news wasn't good. They had misplaced the film and simply missed getting in that month's issue. As my anger rose, I asked what they would do to make things right with me and my client. "We'll run it next month for free," he said confidently.

I knew that wasn't good enough for my client. I couldn't call him and simply say that the ad would run next month. Instead, I insisted that the magazine write a cover letter and supply 1,000 copies of the ad to be used in a direct mailing to my client's target audience among their readers. The publication agreed and then I was able to call the client with the bad news...and the good news. As a result, not only was I not blamed for the mishap, but I also had an opportunity to show how much I cared for my client and was looking out for his interests. That's how to build a long-lasting relationship.

Over the years I bought thousands of dollars of printing services from a variety of printers, some small and some very large. The salespeople I worked with were, for the most part, dedicated and knowledgeable. I had a simple test for my printers-How well could they handle a problem?

At one time, I worked for a small Irishman who seemed to be mad at the world. His only redeeming quality was a reverence for anything Irish, especially his favorite color – green. He had a certain shade of green that had to be on every brochure I printed. It had to match his green precisely. Whenever I gave a printer a job I told them up-front that the green was the most important part of the entire printing job. As you might guess, the green was not always perfect and didn't meet my boss's inspection. It only took me one mistake to vow that I would never present a "bad" green again.

On one particular job, the printer came back with an obviously mismatched green color. I told him it was not acceptable and refused the order. He told me I was wrong to be so picky and that he had no intention of taking the printing back. I had no intention of giving the bad printing job to my boss. We eventually settled on a partial payment for a rerun of the job, but that was the last job I ever gave to that printer. He had not only done a bad printing job but he refused to accept responsibility for it. That is how to end a relationship very quickly.

## No Surprises

Hand-in-hand with accepting total responsibility is an absolute commitment to avoid surprising your customers in any negative way. Probably the most common area for surprises is billing. Unexpected charges, cost overruns, extras or other surprises can be one-way tickets to being fired. I always have made it a personal obligation to review billing for my clients before the accounting department mailed the invoice. In many instances I have found mistakes that would have sent my clients through the roof.

I have also been a buyer of various business products and services throughout my career. To me, the biggest transgression was failure to meet an agreed upon delivery or completion date. Nothing angered me more and sent me looking for new suppliers more quickly. I'm referring to incidents in which I was never told something was going to be late or a problem had arisen. The critical date came and there was no explanation or attempt to alert me. Many times, a simple call would have been enough and would have given me cover when my superiors asked me about the situation. Never, never allow your customer to face his or her management without an explanation about your tardiness.

As I said above, mistakes and misunderstandings will occur. Just be sure you tell your customers about them before they are confronted with a situation that puts them in a bad light to their superiors. Be proactive. Don't shun your obligation to keep your customers' needs uppermost in your mind.

## Expand Your Number of Contacts at Each Client

I always loved to be referred to as "the ad guy" by my client's colleagues because that meant I was becoming synonymous with my function for that company. I took it as the highest form of compliment. It also meant I was recognized by people other than my immediate contact. I figured the more people that knew me, the better my position.

Increasing the number of contacts you have within your client companies can be fairly easy. One of the best ways is through food. A printer that worked with my agency used donuts to do this. Whenever he visited us, he would drop off a dozen donuts in the lunchroom. He became the "printer with the donuts." But that wasn't enough recognition for him. At first he had a little sign that said, "Thanks for the business from XYZ Printing." Then, one day he brought the donuts in a special box that had graphics simulating the exterior of his print shop. It was such a great idea that the salesperson eventually quit selling for the printer and founded his own company to market the special donut boxes to other salespeople. You can order them yourself from www.DonutBox.com. In today's diet conscious world, you might want to consider bagels and schmeer instead of donuts, but the thought is the same and the boxes fit bagels as well.

Food is always a wonderful way to say thanks for business. I used a photographer who always celebrated Valentines Day by sending his clients a giant cookie. And while the days of sending a bottle of Jack Daniels to a client for Christmas are definitely long past, a food item (but not fruitcake!) is almost always appropriate, especially if others can share it in the office.

---

### Introvert Alert

Want to increase the number of people that know you in a client's office but feel unsure about how to do it? Let donuts do the talking. When you show up with a dozen donuts people will be appreciative and remember your kind gesture. If there is a central lunchroom, stay around and have a cup of coffee. Everyone will be asking, "Who brought the donuts?" and you can meet people in a friendly, low pressure atmosphere.

---

## Treat Your Customers Like Prospects

Happily, most relationships run smoothly. Products are delivered on time, services fulfill a need and everything looks peachy. Watch out! This is a dangerous situation.

The more successful you are with a client, the greater the need to guard against complacency. The answer is simple. Treat your clients like prospects. Remember how interested you were during the sales process? You clipped articles out of magazines, called on a regular basis, and asked how the golf game went over the weekend. Just keep doing all of those little things after you've made the sale. The last thing a customer wants is to be taken for granted. If you don't show any interest, you can bet there are competitors who will show a lot of interest. And if you think you don't have time to take care of your customers, just think how much time it would take to replace them.

## Build Personal Relationships

We talked about this earlier as one of the Six Pillars of Introvert Sales Success. All the reasons for building a relationship with a prospect are just as important with a client. In fact, it is even more important now that you presumably have access to the people you want to build relationships with and are part of their team. Review the Murphy's 25 list of important pieces of information to have about your prospects and clients. Fill in any information you may not have yet and find even more facts about your clients. Remember, people like to work with people they like, and they like people who are interested in them.

## Become Part of Your Customer's Team

Once we have climbed the sales mountain and achieved our sales objective, we enter a new phase of our relationship with the customer. We're part of the team and should act like it. Sprinkle conversations with "we" as in "How did we end up the second quarter?" (This is ok for a public company, out of place for a private one). Where not prohibited by law as in accounting relationships, buy at least one share of stock in your customers' companies. You'll receive annual reports and keep abreast of internal information.

If you are in a position where you spend your client's money, always treat their money as you would yours. This does not have to be a conflict of interest. I am firmly convinced the best way to increase income from an account is to treat them fairly and honestly, with an eye toward building a long-lasting relationship. Attempting to maximize short-term income at the expense of your long-term prospects is the stuff of yesterday's selling environment. Be part of your customer's team and you won't have to fear being benched.

**Be on the lookout for new business for your client.**

Just as we all love referrals, your clients like them too. Always be thinking like a salesperson for your customers. For instance, I had a client who manufactured grips for bicycles, exercise equipment and lawn tools. When I bought a new exercise bike and the grips started to fall apart in only a couple of months, I took it to my client and told him that there might be a need for his heavy duty grips on this equipment. It led to an order from the bike manufacturer. That's what I mean by thinking about your customers.

It comes down to having a stake in your customer's success. No matter what you sell, put yourself on your customer's team and let them know it.

## Keep in Touch

As a result of a short-term profit mentality, salespeople are expected to be continually writing orders or, in the case of many professionals, accumulating billable time. This creates a disincentive to keep in touch with clients that may be between buying cycles or otherwise not immediately expected to purchase something from you. Don't fall into this trap. Find ways to keep in touch with your customers. As we discussed, a dozen donuts is a great way to keep your company name in front of clients. Stop by their offices once or twice a month with a morning treat for the troops. Send special event cards, not just Christmas cards. Send Thanksgiving cards, Groundhog Day cards or anything else that is unusual and memorable. What about some flowers for your customer's lobby once or twice a year?

The flip side of keeping in touch is being available to answer questions and getting back to clients quickly when they call. Technology has raised expectations so much that most clients expect a call within minutes or hours at most. Be sure you have procedures in place to allow your customers to contact you and that you return calls in a timely fashion.

### Ask "How Am I Doing?"

Former New York City Mayor Ed Koch was known for walking the streets of the city and asking people, "How Am I Doing." The image of such a powerful and important person taking the time to get "everyman's" opinion made a terrific impact on me. It's simple, direct and powerful. That's the kind of feedback we all should seek from our constituents, our customers.

Today, most companies use satisfaction surveys to gauge their success in meeting customers needs. I use surveys at the end of my seminars to ask attendees if I have fulfilled their expectations and to guide me in preparing future seminars. But that's not enough. Most surveys simply ask for a rating in each of a number of categories and for any comments the individual may want to include. The surveys are designed to be completed quickly, not to elicit useful information. That's why I prefer personal contact in addition to collecting forms. For me, that means talking to as many people as possible after my seminars, asking what worked and what didn't work, what information they expected but didn't get and if they would attend another seminar.

That approach accomplishes two things. It is an early-warning system for problems that can't be explained on the quickie survey and it also shows my personal concern for their satisfaction. Any salesperson can and should do the same. Simply ask. Don't drop any surveys or other feedback programs you may be using, but from time to time personally call your customers and ask how the relationship is going. Done in a friendly, conversational tone, this can be a powerful relationship builder.

## Be Enthusiastic

This can sometimes be very difficult, especially with smaller clients or small assignments from big clients. The longer we work with customers, the more we may take them for granted. The order that once filled us with excitement is now expected. The yearly plan is a chore. If you feel a lack of enthusiasm, it probably shows to your customer, and there are always plenty of competitors who would love to show your customers how much they want their business.

Take a few moments before visiting a current customer. Think back to how you felt when you first received their business. Think how important this assignment or product is to someone in that organization. Be enthusiastic and let it show. You'll find your enthusiasm is contagious and your customers will remain enthused about you.

## Summary

There is nothing more gratifying than having your customer give you additional business because they are so happy with what you have provided to them previously. When I was an account executive in St. Louis, I began working with a division of a Fortune 500 company, one of the largest in the area. After about six months, I began to work with another division of the corporation, and then a few months later, a third division asked me to work on their account. I believe my devotion to the tips I shared with you above accounted for my success. Complacency can be a tough foe but vigilance can pay great dividends.

# Chapter 17

# Selling Additional Products or Services to Current Clients

This has always been one of the greatest areas of concern in any marketing organization. Every marketing plan mentions selling more of the same products to existing clients and finding other products to sell to these same customers. It should be easy. But most times the goal of getting additional sales remains a source of frustration for management and sales people alike.

In the accounting business, managers hated to hear of one of our audit clients giving a major consulting assignment to a competitor. It was not uncommon for the customer to say they didn't know we offered that particular product or service, and, as a consequence, didn't even consider us. An electric products company I worked with spent a tremendous amount of time and energy trying to sell lighting, motors and controls to a group of customers. Some bought lighting, some motors, and some controls. The trick was trying to get them to buy all three from one source. Here are some ideas on how to sell more.

## Keep Your Eyes and Ears Open

If information is power, you have power with your existing clients. In the course of providing your product or service, you will be exposed to the inner workings of your client and often see opportunities to provide additional solutions to problems that the customer may not even see. The accounting business is a great example of such opportunities. In the course of their work, accountants often uncover problems that need attention. Junior staff members are instructed to bring potential problems to the attention of the engagement manager who alerts the client. In some case the auditor can provide the solution. In other cases, the auditors may not have a solution but still win the admiration of the client for "being on the team."

Another example of this occurred with one of my advertising clients. While sitting in the lobby one day, I noticed some of their displays were seriously outdated and photos showed old equipment. I drew up a sketch of a new display idea and offered it to my surprised contact. My agency didn't build the new displays but we did supervise photography and provide graphics for them. More business from an existing client.

## New Products and New Ideas

Sitting back and waiting for your client to call you with additional orders is a prescription for a selling disaster. Remember that you're part of a team and your function is to provide a steady stream of products and ideas to keep your customer competitive. Just as you looked upon your initial sales call as an opportunity to provide a solution to a problem, your delivery of new products and ideas does the same thing.

In my experience, the problem is often to match your client with your company's products and services. The larger the company you work for, the more difficult this can be. There may be so many product offerings that it becomes an overwhelming task to find those that best fit your clients' needs.

It was for just such a dilemma that Deloitte & Touche instituted a tax program called the Client Service Matrix. New tax saving ideas are shared across the Firm with client service professionals, who are asked to review each idea for applicability to individual clients. As a result, tax sales people have a steady stream of cost-saving ideas for their customers.

If you are not part of a large firm, you have to find these opportunties yourself. Review your company's product offering against your client's needs. Don't find out your client just bought a competing product or service because they didn't know you had a comparable or superior alternative.

The other point is always to bring new ideas to your customers. Don't wait for them to ask. The more dynamic your market, the more you need to be constantly at their door with innovations. For instance, over the last decade, the advertising business has changed from being a supplier of ads and media time to an integrator of print, electronic, digital and interactive media. Agencies that weren't at the forefront of this change, leading their clients into this new technology, have gone to that great agency in the sky.

An advertising agency in St. Louis is a great example of what can happen when a company allows its clients to move past them in the use of technology. The management of this agency was slow to adapt to the use of computer technology in areas other than billing. When its largest client, a major bank planning to expand significantly, asked for assistance in database marketing, the agency president was unable to respond and quickly lost the respect of the bank's marketing staff. Within a few months, the bank moved to another agency, one known for its database capabilities and use of technology in all aspects of agency operations. Within a few short years, the technophobe agency closed and the president retired.

## Summary

Keeping present clients and selling more to them is an important part of sales. As more companies recognize the financial advantages of retaining their present customers compared to spending to find new customers, servicing accounts is given a higher priority in the organization. Sales people with introvert personality traits can be very successful at retaining customers by relying on their knowledge, dedication to customer service and detail orientation. These skills are much more valuable when applied to keeping customers, compared to the skills more often associated with gregarious extroverts.

# Chapter 18

# Selling Skills Self-Assessment Revisited

Your commitment of time and energy to read this book is hopefully accompanied by a commitment to make real changes in the way you look at yourself, your business and your customers. Let's take another look at the Selling Skills Self-Assessment, focusing on what we've learned and what we can do to build on the information we've explored.

**1. Selling is an enjoyable part of my business life.**

It really can be. Over the years, selling has introduced me to a great number of really nice people. A few were not so nice. But by far most were interesting, intelligent individuals dedicated to doing their absolute best at their jobs, for their business, for their customers and for their families. When you are honest with yourself, most people instinctively understand it. On the other hand, if you are not being honest with yourself, if you are trying to be what you are not, your customers will sense this also and react negatively. Once you have aligned your actions with your core beliefs and see your selling as providing solutions to people's business and personal needs, selling can be enjoyable — and maybe even fun.

**2. I see myself as a knowledgeable expert with information and ideas that will help my customers.**

This is really the key to successful selling for introverts. It takes the burden off "pushing" something on someone or attempting to trick people into making hasty or wrong decisions. Base your selling on your expertise and you will be successful. If you are selling something you aren't an expert at yet, become one. Study, study, study and you can be an expert passing on information to others. Many of the best salespeople find that helping others and making money have an uncanny ability to come together, providing satisfaction and financial gain in great quantities.

3. **I do at least some research on a company before making a sales contact.**

The very best salespeople create their own contact forms. Some of the information is filled in before they make a sales call and some is filled in during the course of the sales call. Make up your own contact form, one that contains all the information that is important for your business. Before you talk to a prospect, you'll have a visual reminder of the data that you need to start off on the right foot and build a win-win relationship.

4. **I view selling as providing solutions to my customers' problems.**

If you recall, I defined a "solution" as a three-part system that combines the basic product or service, the after-the-sale service and finally a value-added component. If you keep the concept of value-added in mind as you strategize on how to approach prospects, you'll automatically focus on customer benefits. The value that you add to your relationship with your customer is what makes you special, what defines your business purpose and unique selling proposition.

5. **I have a written plan for sales calls and review my performance after each meeting.**

This can be a real eye-opener. I admit that through most of

my selling life I never had a written plan or seriously reviewed my performance in meetings other than to follow-up on action items. Then, one day I read about the positive contributions a written plan can make to selling. Now, I take a few minutes to write three or four objective for every meeting in a small notebook I carry. Then immediately after the sales call I review the objectives and note what I accomplished and, just as importantly, what I failed to do. Over a period of time, patterns emerge for good or bad. You can build on your good actions and work on your bad. For instance, I went through a period when I consistently neglected to get a definite commitment on the time my client would require to approve advertising copy. As a result, there was confusion between me and my client that added precious time to completing projects. Based on the knowledge I gained about my neglecting this important practice, I made it one of my goals for each meeting and was able to walk away from my client with definite commitments.

**6. I know the real benefits my products/services provide for my customers.**

One of the keys to introvert selling success is believing in your own mind that what you are offering to your customer provides him or her with real, tangible value. The way to get to that value is to thoroughly understand the benefits the customer will reap by parting with their money, and of course communicating that benefit to the customer. We all know the difference between features and benefits, but ask yourself if you really feel your customers will enjoy those benefits. Once you have that commitment in your own mind, it will be much easier to communicate it to your prospects.

**7. When I leave a prospect's office or home, I have a reason to contact that person again.**

This one can be difficult. Too often I've heard salespeople end a sales call with, "When can I call you again" or "When is a good time to check back?" When they do call back, there is no natural opening to the conversation other than the feeble, "Have you made a decision yet" or "I wanted to check in and see how things were going." Try this instead. As you plan your meeting, write down the four or five main points you want to make with your listener and then prioritize them. Take the bottom one and any substantiating materials and put them away. Don't use them but keep them in the "bullpen" for the late innings of the sales process. Make your sales call and tell your prospect you will follow with even more information. That creates your follow-up.

**8. I know more than one person at each of my customer locations.**

By now, this should be a priority at every account you possess. Nothing makes you more vulnerable than having one contact. Review the suggestions I made for broadening your contacts in Chapter 16. Pay particular attention to your contact's immediate subordinate and to others on the same level. One day they could be your lifelines to the account.

**9. I look for other products/services to sell to my existing clients.**

No other tactic can lead to quicker increases in sales. As I advised, the best way to find out if there are opportunities is by asking about their problems and frustrations. As you build your relationships with clients, you'll find them more than willing to open up about their needs. Then find those that you or your company can fulfill. Be creative. Make asking about other opportunities part of your pre-meeting list of objectives for every account.

**10. I know my sales contact's education, hobbies, hometown, family status and pets.**

This may seem like an invasion of privacy to some, but it

really is good selling. Having something to talk about can make even the most introverted of us much more comfortable. Make a "Murphy's 25" list for each of your current clients and prospects, today. If you simply start to ask the right questions but don't formalize the process and write it all down, you'll find yourself confused and less-than-smooth in your presentation.

**11. I adjust my voice and actions to fit my listener.**

Have you focused on this during a sales call? Listen closely to your prospect/customer and become aware of how loudly they speak, how quickly they speak and the forcefulness they use to make their points. Then try to complement them by speaking in a similar way. The same goes for movements. If the speaker uses hand movements, then try to use some also. If they move closer as they speak, try to move closer to them when you speak.

**12. I can explain my product or service and the benefits it offers in 30 seconds or less.**

This is one of the highlights of my seminars. I have attendees pair off and practice their WOW statements on each other. Then the receivers critique their partners to the rest of the seminar. It is amazing how this simple exercise can help people focus on the true benefits they offer their customers. I urge you to develop your WOW statement and use it every opportunity you can. You'll find you will look forward to meeting new people and telling them about yourself.

**13. I prepare my voice mail messages in advance in case the person I am calling is not available.**

Just recently I broke my own rule and was reminded of how important this simple habit can be. I had received a voice mail message from someone at a very large local company. They were interested in a selling seminar and wanted more details. In my rush and excitement to get back to them, I didn't prepare, on paper or mentally, a message. Having just received the call I thought the person would be available and I could discuss my program with her. Instead I was connected to her voice mail and, although I left a good message, it wasn't up to my exacting standards. I'll try to follow my own advice more closely in the future.

**14. I never take rejection personally.**

If you've been in selling for any time, you've probably dealt successfully with rejection. If you are still new to selling, you must learn to separate yourself from your customer's decision to buy or not buy. If you don't, you'll wind up bitter and disillusioned, and cut yourself off from any hope of real success.

**15. I think a sales call on a new prospect is an opportunity to meet a new person and learn about a new company.**

When you find yourself looking forward to selling and meeting new people, you know you are on the road to success. Although I still consider myself an introvert, over the years I have learned to appreciate meeting new people to the point that I can truthfully say selling is one of my favorite activities. But let me add that most of my direct selling activities are successful because I have an active sales "farming" program bringing me prospects.

**16. I have an active personal marketing program in place.**

I've given you a number of alternatives for your personal marketing plan. Whether it be speaking before groups, networking, using advertising and public relations or becoming active in organizations, you need to find what works for you…and do it continually. Your "seeds" will bear fruit if you tend your soil on a steady basis.

**17. On a sales call, I listen more than talk.**

This was probably the easiest question to answer "yes" to for true introverts. But be sure not to overdo the listening. There is such a concept as too quiet for your own good. Listen closely, but also be sure to make your thoughts and expertise known at the appropriate times.

## 18. I consistently look for signs that a prospect is ready to buy.

At times it can be easy to get so enmeshed in our sales presentation that we don't know when to stop and simply ask for the sale. I've seen sales people who were nervous completely forget about their listener and stumble right past clear signs that the customer was ready to buy. Be sure to keep an eye on your customer and move to make the sale when you see the buying signs we discussed earlier.

# Afterword

Thank you for buying and reading this book. It is my sincere desire that you will benefit both personally and professionally from the time you have spent reading and completing the exercises.

I would appreciate hearing your opinions on the thoughts and techniques contained in Successful Selling for Introverts, plus some of your experiences in putting the book into action. I would also be happy to answer any further questions you may have.

You can contact me at my web site: www.introvertsales.com.

Good selling!

To order additional copies of *Successful Selling for Introverts* call 503-516-3193.